CELTIC SEERSHIP

Navigating Otherworldly Visions
in the Modern Age

D.R. T STEPHENS

S.D.N Publishing

Copyright © 2023 S.D.N Publishing

All rights reserved

The characters and events portrayed in this book are fictitious. Any similarity to real persons, living or dead, is coincidental and not intended by the author.

No part of this book may be reproduced, or stored in a retrieval system, or transmitted in any form or by any means, electronic, mechanical, photocopying, recording, or otherwise, without express written permission of the publisher.

ISBN: 9798860308626

CONTENTS

Title Page
Copyright
General Disclaimer   1
Chapter 1: Introduction: The Legacy of Celtic Seers   3
Chapter 2: Historical Overview: Druids, Bards, and Seers   7
Chapter 3: The Otherworld: Realms Beyond the Veil   11
Chapter 4: Interactions with the Fae   15
Chapter 5: Tools of the Seer: Ogham, Runes, and Divination   19
Chapter 6: Sacred Texts and Lore   23
Chapter 7: Visions and Prophecies: Gifts of the Sight   26
Chapter 8: Sacred Landscapes: Stone Circles and Ancient Sites   30
Chapter 9: Elemental Magic and Seership   34
Chapter 10: Festivals and Rituals: Celebrating the Celtic Wheel of the Year   38
Chapter 11: Connecting with Celtic Deities   42
Chapter 12: The Role of Ancestor Worship   46
Chapter 13: Modern Seership: Balancing Tradition and Innovation   50
Chapter 14: The Role of Nature: Trees, Animals, and Spirits   53
Chapter 15: Animal Totems and Familiars   57

Chapter 16: Dreaming the Celtic Way: Visions and Insights	61
Chapter 17: Oracles and Channeling: Messages from Beyond	65
Chapter 18: The Role of Herbs and Plants	69
Chapter 19: Overcoming Challenges: Ethical Considerations in Seership	72
Chapter 20: Navigating Transitions: Life, Death, and Rebirth	76
Chapter 21: The Psychology of Seership	79
Chapter 22: Sacred Geometry and Symbols	82
Chapter 23: The Importance of Music and Chanting	85
Chapter 24: Gender Roles in Celtic Seership	88
Chapter 25: Astral Projection and Out-of-Body Experiences	91
Chapter 26: The Future of Celtic Seership: Emerging Trends	97
Chapter 27: Personal Journeys: Stories of Modern Celtic Seers	100
Chapter 28: Online Communities and Digital Seership	103
Chapter 29: Environmental Stewardship and Seership	106
Chapter 30: Creating Your Own Tools and Rituals	109
Chapter 31: Secrecy and Mystery Schools	112
Chapter 32: Children and Seership	115
Chapter 33: Teaching and Mentoring in Seership	118
Chapter 34: Seership and the Wider Occult Tradition	122
Chapter 35: Conclusion: Navigating the Path Ahead	126
THE END	129

GENERAL DISCLAIMER

This book is intended to provide general information to the reader on the topics covered. The author and publisher have made every effort to ensure that the information herein is accurate and up-to-date at the time of publication. However, they do not warrant or guarantee the accuracy, completeness, adequacy, or currency of the information contained in this book. The author and publisher expressly disclaim any liability or responsibility for any errors or omissions in the content herein.

The information, guidance, advice, tips, and suggestions provided in this book are not intended to replace professional advice or consultation. Readers are strongly encouraged to consult with an appropriate professional for specific advice tailored to their situation before making any decisions or taking any actions based on the content of this book.

The views and opinions expressed in this book are those of the author and do not necessarily reflect the official policy or position of any other agency, organization, employer or company.

The author and publisher are not responsible for any actions taken or not taken by the reader based on the information, advice, or suggestions provided in this book. The reader is solely responsible for their actions and the consequences thereof.

This book is not intended to be a source of legal, business, medical or psychological advice, and readers are cautioned to seek the services of a competent professional in these or other areas of expertise.

All product names, logos, and brands are property of their respective owners. All company, product and service names used in this book are for identification purposes only. Use of these names, logos, and brands does not imply endorsement.

Readers of this book are advised to do their own due diligence when it comes to making decisions and all information, products, services and advice that have been provided should be independently verified by your own qualified professionals.

By reading this book, you agree that the author and publisher are not responsible for your success or failure resulting from any information presented in this book.

CHAPTER 1: INTRODUCTION: THE LEGACY OF CELTIC SEERS

Brief Overview

The enigmatic landscape of Celtic Seership stretches like an evergreen forest—dense, magical, and filled with arcane wisdom. This chapter serves as an introduction to the vast and intricate tapestry that constitutes the art and practice of Celtic Seership. From its rich historical context to its relevance in modern society, the role of the Celtic seer is a potent blend of tradition, vision, and communion with the natural world. Whether you are a seasoned practitioner or a curious wanderer stepping onto this mystical path for the first time, understanding the legacy of Celtic seers is a crucial starting point.

The Historical Significance

The practice of Seership is as ancient as the Celtic culture itself. Seers, or "fáith" in Old Irish, have been prominent figures in Celtic society for centuries. With origins in pre-Christian times, these individuals were deeply respected and sought-after for their ability to peer into hidden realms, offer prophetic guidance, and interpret natural signs and omens. Druids, bards, and seers formed a hierarchical system of spiritual and intellectual authority. Druids were often philosophers, legal experts, and ritual specialists, while bards were musicians and poets who chronicled history and lore. Seers, however, occupied a unique place in this system. They specialized in divination, healing, and the navigation of the Otherworld—the metaphysical realm that is home to deities, spirits, and other supernatural entities.

Bridging the Gap: From Antiquity to Modernity

The passage of time has not diminished the allure of Celtic Seership; rather, it has evolved to meet the needs of contemporary society. Modern practitioners still employ age-old techniques such as Ogham divination, working with runes, or interpreting the natural world for omens and signs. But they also embrace new modalities like tarot cards and even digital divination tools. The constant interplay between tradition and innovation reflects the adaptive nature of this practice.

The Natural World and Beyond

One of the defining characteristics of Celtic Seership is its profound connection to the natural world. Trees, animals, rivers, and even celestial bodies are not just passive elements; they are active participants in the divinatory process. In Celtic cosmology, the natural world is a tangible extension of the Otherworld, acting as a medium through which messages, insights, and visions are relayed. This intimate relationship with nature distinguishes Celtic Seership from other forms of divination and augury.

Accessibility in the Modern Age

In our contemporary setting, the call to Seership is not limited to those with a Celtic background or those initiated through secret traditions. With the democratization of knowledge through books, online courses, and communities, Celtic Seership has become more accessible than ever. However, the sacred essence of the practice remains protected, often requiring sincere dedication, study, and ethical commitment.

A Practice for All Seasons

Celtic Seership is not merely a set of esoteric techniques; it's a way of life. It demands a holistic approach that considers ethical conduct, psychological awareness, and a deep respect for both the seen and unseen worlds. The festivals and rituals that mark the Celtic Wheel of the Year serve as regular touchpoints for reflection and growth, allowing practitioners to keep their skills and insights attuned to the rhythms of nature.

A Journey Into the Profound

As we navigate the chapters that follow, you will encounter a wealth of information designed to guide, enlighten, and challenge you. From the complexities of the Otherworld to the modern-day ethics of being a seer, each chapter builds upon this foundational understanding of what it means to walk the path of a Celtic seer. The journey promises to be as enriching as it is enlightening, revealing layers of ancient wisdom tailored for contemporary seekers.

This chapter has aimed to illuminate the legacy of Celtic seers, setting the stage for a deeper exploration into their history, practices, and evolving role in the modern world. The timeless wisdom of Celtic seership beckons, inviting us to step forward into a world that seamlessly blends the mystical with the practical, the ancient with the modern, and the earthly with the otherworldly.

CHAPTER 2: HISTORICAL OVERVIEW: DRUIDS, BARDS, AND SEERS

To fully understand the practice of Celtic Seership, one must delve into the origins of its primary facilitators: Druids, Bards, and Seers. These roles are foundational elements in the Celtic spiritual tradition and have shaped the contours of Celtic culture and religion for centuries. By exploring their historical context and functional relevance, you can gain a rich understanding of how Seership is grounded in both antiquity and modernity.

The Druids: Spiritual Leaders and Advisors

The Druids were the intellectual and spiritual elite of ancient Celtic society, playing an array of roles from judges to teachers and from philosophers to ritual facilitators. Often described as the "wise men" or "high priests" of the Celts, the Druids were responsible for overseeing religious rituals, adjudicating disputes, and preserving the lore and knowledge of their people. Historically, their training took many years and encompassed a broad range of subjects including astronomy, mathematics, law, and natural philosophy.

Their role was not just limited to the temporal realm. Druids were believed to have profound insights into the Otherworld, making them essential figures in guiding the society's spiritual direction. Their understanding of sacred landscapes, herbal remedies, and divination made them the perfect conduits for messages from beyond the veil, establishing the earliest practices that would later evolve into formal Seership.

The Bards: Storytellers and Keepers of Tradition

While Druids were the wise scholars and spiritual advisors, Bards were the storytellers, musicians, and poets of Celtic society. They held the crucial role of preserving history, myths, and legends through the oral tradition. Often, they were trained by Druids in the arts of memory, poetry, and music.

The role of the Bard was not just that of an entertainer. Through their storytelling, they also acted as custodians of social norms, values, and collective memory. Their tales often contained teachings and prophecies, serving as another medium through which Seership was manifested. The power of the spoken word was immensely potent in Celtic society, and Bards were among the first to use this power to convey messages from other realms.

The Seers: Visionaries and Prophets

Seers were the visionaries of Celtic society, often working in conjunction with Druids and Bards but specializing in divination, visions, and prophecies. They were the masters of "second sight," a form of extrasensory perception that allowed them to foresee events, interact with otherworldly beings, and navigate realms beyond the earthly plane. Their role was primarily diagnostic and prescriptive; they identified imbalances in both the spiritual and material worlds and offered solutions to rectify them.

The methods employed by seers were diverse, ranging from dream interpretation and scrying to reading omens in nature. Ogham sticks, runes, and various forms of divination were tools often used by seers for their practices, which will be discussed in more detail in a later chapter.

A Symbiotic Relationship

It is essential to understand that these roles often overlapped and were not mutually exclusive. A Druid could also be a seer, and a Bard might have seer-like abilities. The lines separating them were not rigid but fluid, emphasizing the interconnectedness of these roles within the framework of Celtic spirituality. Each group contributed to a collective spiritual wisdom, working in harmony to ensure the spiritual and material well-being of their communities.

In today's context, the roles of Druids, Bards, and Seers have adapted to contemporary needs. Yet, the essence of their functions remains intact, rooted in the ancient principles that once governed Celtic society. Many modern practitioners wear multiple hats, blending the wisdom of these roles to develop a holistic approach to Celtic Seership.

Summary

The roles of Druids, Bards, and Seers were integral to the Celtic world, serving as the main conduits of religious, social, and spiritual wisdom. While they each had their unique responsibilities and methods, their functions were interconnected, reflecting a complex but harmonious system of beliefs and practices. Understanding their roles and relationships provides a necessary foundation for exploring the intricacies of Celtic Seership, which has both ancient roots and modern branches. This symbiotic relationship among the Druids, Bards, and Seers is a testament to the rich and complex tapestry of Celtic spirituality, a tradition that continues to flourish and adapt in the modern age.

CHAPTER 3: THE OTHERWORLD: REALMS BEYOND THE VEIL

As we delve deeper into the enigmatic universe of Celtic Seership, understanding the Otherworld is essential. This mysterious realm, often described as lying "beyond the veil" of our ordinary reality, is a cornerstone of Celtic spirituality and a focal point for seers. With its own distinct physical laws and entities, the Otherworld is both intriguing and complex. In this chapter, we will unpack what the Otherworld means in Celtic belief systems, how it differs from our tangible reality, and its overarching significance to the practice of Seership.

What is the Otherworld?

The concept of an "Otherworld" is present in various spiritual traditions, but it holds a special place in Celtic cosmology. In Celtic beliefs, the Otherworld is a parallel realm that coexists with our physical world but operates on different metaphysical principles. It's a domain of gods, spirits, and other supernatural entities including the infamous Fae. The realm is often described as wondrous yet perilous, filled with both incredible beauty and inherent danger.

While the Otherworld is thought to be separate, it is intrinsically connected to our world. Natural phenomena like the changing seasons, eclipses, or even the mysterious appearance of mist are sometimes considered "thin places" where the veil between the two realms is particularly porous. In ancient tales, it's common for heroes or mortals to accidentally or intentionally cross into the Otherworld, often facing trials, receiving gifts, or acquiring wisdom before returning.

The Rules of the Realm

The Otherworld operates on its own set of laws that defy our conventional understanding of physics and time. In many stories and teachings, time flows differently there—what may seem like days in the Otherworld could equate to years in our realm. This discrepancy has been cited in multiple folktales, where unwitting visitors to the Otherworld return to find that much time has passed in their absence.

Additionally, the concept of "geasa" (singular "geis") is important. These are taboos or obligations that must be followed in the Otherworld; breaking them often results in dire consequences. This underlines the need for anyone who navigates these realms, especially seers, to have a deep understanding and respect for its laws.

Seers as Navigators

For seers, the Otherworld is not just a concept but a practical aspect of their spiritual work. They are considered navigators who can safely traverse this realm, either in a shamanistic journey, a dream, or a vision. Their role is to interact with the entities that reside there, to obtain wisdom, healing properties, or even prophecies that can be applied in the physical world. Seers often serve as intermediaries, bridging the gap between the corporeal and the Otherworldly, a role that comes with both honor and responsibilities.

Rituals and Protection

For a seer to enter the Otherworld, specific rituals and protections are often required. The use of protective talismans, chanting of ancient incantations, and the drawing of sacred symbols are common practices. These rituals are not mere pageantry but serve as shields and guides in a realm where the unprepared can easily become lost or ensnared. The exact nature of these rituals varies, often personalized by the seer's own experiences and teachings, but the need for them is nearly universal.

Relevance in Modern Seership

In our contemporary understanding, the Otherworld remains an essential aspect of the practice. The modern seer still engages with this realm, albeit often in a manner adapted to fit new paradigms and understandings. Technologies like guided meditations and virtual reality are being explored as tools to assist in these journeys, but the foundational respect for the Otherworld's intricacies remains steadfast. Today's seers are as much explorers of this realm as their ancient predecessors, seeking wisdom and insight that benefit both individual and community.

In summary, the Otherworld is a cornerstone of Celtic spirituality and Seership. It is a parallel realm rich in complexity, governed by its own rules, and populated by entities both benevolent and malevolent. The role of the seer as a navigator of this realm is both a privileged and precarious one, requiring in-depth knowledge, respect, and preparation. As we continue to explore the various facets of Celtic Seership, the enduring relevance of the Otherworld serves as a constant reminder of the depth and diversity of this ancient yet ever-evolving practice.

CHAPTER 4: INTERACTIONS WITH THE FAE

Celtic Seership is a practice rich with interactions that go beyond the mundane world we typically perceive. One of the most captivating elements of this tradition is the seer's relationship with the Fae, the magical beings that occupy the realm of folklore and myth in Celtic tradition. Understanding these interactions enriches the depth and complexity of Seership, serving as a bridge between our world and the Otherworld.

The Nature of the Fae

In Celtic mythology, the Fae are often considered nature spirits that dwell in the wilderness, bodies of water, or ancient sites. They are as diverse as nature itself, encompassing beings that can be both benevolent and malevolent. In folklore, the Fae may be categorized into various subtypes, such as the leprechaun, the banshee, or the selkie. These magical entities share common characteristics, like a deep connection to natural elements and a knack for shape-shifting, but each type has its unique qualities.

The Fae are not merely mythical characters in stories; they are considered a part of the animistic worldview of the Celts, wherein all natural things have spirits. As such, the interaction with these entities is not seen as metaphorical but rather as a very tangible aspect of a seer's journey. These spirits often serve as guides, guardians, or mentors to seers who venture into the Otherworld or seek wisdom in their divination practices.

Seers and the Fae: A Mutual Relationship

For seers, interaction with the Fae can be a two-way street. The Fae may seek out the seer to deliver messages or offer assistance. Conversely, seers may call upon specific types of Fae to help in their quests for wisdom, healing, or transformation. Traditional rituals, invocations, and offerings are used to attract the Fae, and once communication is established, the seer must be respectful and cautious. These beings are known for their tricks and their intricate social norms, and offending a faery can result in misfortune.

Moreover, the relationship with the Fae is often initiated through rites of passage or certain milestone experiences in a seer's development. These can include intense visionary experiences, dream encounters, or even real-world synchronicities that are too potent to ignore. Once this relationship is established, it often becomes a long-lasting partnership, with the Fae serving various roles, from healer to muse to protector.

Offerings and Rituals

Part of nurturing a relationship with the Fae involves rituals and offerings. It is customary to leave offerings of milk, honey, or bread at sites considered to be faery haunts, like ancient stones, wells, or groves. This serves as a gesture of goodwill and opens the channels for mutual cooperation. Rituals may include singing, dancing, and the use of specific herbs known to attract faery folk, like lavender or thyme. These rituals not only honor the Fae but also fortify the seer's connection to the natural world.

Lessons from the Fae

One of the most valuable aspects of interaction with the Fae is the lessons they offer. Whether in the form of riddles, parables, or direct advice, the wisdom imparted often contains deep ecological, spiritual, and ethical dimensions. They might teach the seer about the medicinal properties of plants, the secrets of natural cycles, or the interconnectedness of all life. In this way, the Fae act as conservators of ancient wisdom, a wisdom deeply tied to the Earth and its processes.

Cautionary Tales

While interactions with the Fae can be enlightening and transformational, they come with their share of risks. It is crucial to approach these beings with the utmost respect and care, mindful of their own rules and customs. There are numerous cautionary tales in folklore about individuals who have misled or disrespected the Fae and suffered consequences. Therefore, for the seer, the integrity and sincerity of the interaction are paramount, as is the need for boundaries.

To summarize, the relationship between Celtic seers and the Fae is a deeply rooted aspect of the tradition, one that serves both practical and spiritual purposes. The Fae act as guides and mentors, helping seers navigate the complexities of the Otherworld and offering insights that can be applied in our reality. By honoring and nurturing this relationship, a seer not only gains valuable allies but also enriches their understanding of the world around them, both seen and unseen.

CHAPTER 5: TOOLS OF THE SEER: OGHAM, RUNES, AND DIVINATION

In the intricate tapestry of Celtic Seership, tools and instruments hold a special place as both aids and representations of wisdom. These tools are not just inanimate objects but vessels that carry the energy and intention behind seership practices. This chapter aims to delve into the different tools employed by seers, their historical contexts, and how they are relevant in modern-day practices.

Ogham: The Alphabet of Trees

Ogham is often referred to as the "Celtic Tree Alphabet" and is deeply rooted in the Celtic tradition. Originally, it was a writing system used for inscriptions on stone and wood but eventually evolved into a system for divination and magic. In the context of Seership, each Ogham stave is linked with a specific tree, and by extension, its associated qualities and meanings. For instance, the Birch symbolizes new beginnings, while the Oak stands for strength and stability.

Using Ogham for divination usually involves casting a set of Ogham staves and interpreting the patterns and combinations in which they fall. These staves can be made of wooden sticks, inscribed with Ogham symbols, or they could be elaborately carved pieces. The modern resurgence in the use of Ogham has also seen it being employed in meditation and as a means of connecting with tree spirits.

Runes: Symbols of Elemental Power

Though often associated more closely with Norse mythology, runes have been used in Celtic practices as well. The Celtic interpretation of runes usually involves a blend of symbolic understanding from both traditions. Runes are alphabetic signs but unlike Ogham, they are associated with elemental powers and concepts rather than specific trees.

Runes can be made of a variety of materials, though stone and wood are the most common. They are usually cast in a similar fashion to Ogham staves and interpreted based on their positions and relationships to each other. Runes may also be used in magical works and are sometimes inscribed onto talismans or used in rituals to invoke specific energies.

Divination Methods: Beyond the Written Word

Apart from Ogham and runes, Celtic seers often use other methods of divination like tarot cards, crystal balls, and pendulums. The tarot, in its various forms, offers a more narrative approach to divination, with cards representing different stages of life or aspects of the human experience.

Crystal balls, or "seer stones," offer a more intuitive form of divination where the seer gazes into the crystal to discern images or symbols. This practice is sometimes referred to as "scrying" and can also be performed with water, fire, or other reflective surfaces.

Pendulums are often used for "yes" or "no" questions and function through the subtle movements caused by the energy fields around them. In Celtic Seership, pendulums may be used in conjunction with a board that has various outcomes written on it, making it a more detailed tool for divination.

Modern Applications: Adapting Tools for Today's World

With the advent of technology, the essence of these ancient tools has been translated into modern formats. Digital versions of Ogham and rune casting apps are available, providing interpretations and guidance at the touch of a button. However, many practitioners believe that the tangible, physical interaction with these tools enhances the depth and authenticity of the seership experience.

It's also worth noting that these tools are not exclusive to Celtic Seership but have been integrated into various other spiritual and magical practices. The universal appeal of these tools lies in their capacity to serve as bridges between the corporeal and the ethereal, the known and the unknown.

Crafting Your Own Tools: A Personal Touch

One of the most rewarding aspects of delving into the practice of

Celtic Seership is crafting your own divination tools. Carving your own Ogham staves or rune stones not only adds a personal touch but also imbues the tool with your own energy, making it a more effective conduit for your intentions.

In closing, tools and instruments in Celtic Seership serve as more than mere accessories. They are partners in a deeply spiritual endeavor, each with their unique qualities and capabilities. Whether ancient or modern, these tools hold the key to unlocking layers of wisdom and offering insights that guide us through the labyrinth of existence.

CHAPTER 6: SACRED TEXTS AND LORE

In the rich tapestry of Celtic Seership, sacred texts and lore hold a special place as vessels of ancient wisdom. These texts inform the practices, rituals, and beliefs that have been passed down through generations. Not merely historical documents, they are living legacies that guide modern practitioners in their spiritual journeys. This chapter delves into the role of these sacred texts and lore, their origins, and their ongoing relevance to the practice of Seership today.

Origins of Sacred Texts and Lore

One may wonder where these mystical writings originated. The Celts did not initially have a written language, so much of their lore was passed down orally. Druids, bards, and seers were responsible for memorizing vast amounts of information, which they then conveyed through storytelling, songs, and rites. It wasn't until the arrival of Christian monks and the usage of written Latin that many of these stories were committed to parchment. Texts like the "Book of Kells" and manuscripts like the "Welsh Triads" offer us valuable insights into these ancient cultures, though they often come through a Christian lens.

The Mabinogion and Mythological Cycles

The Mabinogion, a Welsh anthology of stories that were later transcribed, is one of the most important sources of Celtic mythology and wisdom. Similarly, Ireland has its Mythological Cycle, Ulster Cycle, and Fenian Cycle, which were eventually written down in manuscripts like the "Book of the Dun Cow" and the "Book of Leinster." These cycles tell stories of gods, heroes, and the Otherworld, providing key insights into the worldview and cosmology of ancient Celts. They contain elements that are central to the practice of Seership, including interactions with the fae, prophecies, and the use of magical items.

The Ogham Alphabet and Divination

In the realm of written symbols, the Ogham stands as a significant part of Celtic heritage. It's an alphabet consisting of a series of lines and is often used in divination. While it's unclear whether the Ogham originated solely for magical or pragmatic purposes, it undoubtedly plays a role in modern Seership. Stones, sticks, or cards marked with Ogham symbols are often used as tools for gaining insight into the past, present, or future. In essence, the Ogham alphabet serves as a link between the written word and the mystical realm, acting as both language and oracle.

The Role of the Druids

The Druids were not just religious leaders but also scholars and keepers of wisdom. While not all their knowledge was written down, they were meticulous in their study and interpretation of lore and texts that were available to them. Even after the decline of Druidic culture due to Roman conquest and Christianization, their influence can be felt in the texts that were written down later. Druidic teachings often filter through, providing an additional layer of understanding to the interpretations of these texts by modern seers.

Sacred Texts in Modern Practice

Today's practitioners draw upon these ancient resources as roadmaps to spiritual insight. Whether it's studying the wisdom contained in the Mabinogion or using Ogham for divination, the relevance of these texts endures. Modern translations and interpretations have made them more accessible, but the essence remains unchanged. They continue to serve as foundational elements in contemporary practices of Celtic Seership, lending historical depth and cultural richness to modern spiritual explorations. Some seers even incorporate these texts into rituals, reading passages as invocations or meditating on the lessons they impart.

In summary, the sacred texts and lore of Celtic tradition offer a deep well of wisdom, serving as invaluable guides to understanding the metaphysical and practical aspects of Seership. Although many texts came to us refracted through the lens of later cultures and religions, their core messages remain potent. Whether one is drawn to the enchanting stories of the Mabinogion or the cryptic symbols of the Ogham alphabet, these age-old texts bridge the gap between the ancient and the modern, enriching the practice of Seership across the ages.

CHAPTER 7: VISIONS AND PROPHECIES: GIFTS OF THE SIGHT

In the complex tapestry of Celtic Seership, visions and prophecies play a vital role. These manifestations of insight are considered as both a gift and a responsibility for the seer. They offer a means to access wisdom, guidance, and foresight, not just for the individual seer but often for the community at large. In this chapter, we will delve into the types of visions experienced, the nature of prophecies, and the ethical considerations surrounding their interpretation and sharing.

Types of Visions

Visions in the context of Celtic Seership can be broadly classified into three categories: intuitive, revelatory, and interactive.

Intuitive Visions: These are spontaneous images or symbols that appear to the seer, often during meditative or contemplative states. They usually require interpretation as they are rich in symbolism rather than literal depictions.

Revelatory Visions: These are clearer, more detailed visions that convey specific information or reveal hidden truths. Often, these are the types of visions associated with prophecies.

Interactive Visions: In these visions, seers find themselves in scenarios where they can interact with beings or elements from the Otherworld. These visions can often be catalysts for deeper personal and spiritual transformation.

The Nature of Prophecies

Prophecy in the Celtic tradition is not merely fortune-telling. It is a nuanced form of spiritual guidance that can encompass warnings, enlightenment, or calls to action. Prophecies can be both personal and communal, affecting an individual's choices or the destiny of entire communities.

It's crucial to note that in the Celtic understanding, prophecy is not considered as predestination. The future is malleable, and prophecies serve as guidances that can influence decision-making but not dictate it. Therefore, the ethical responsibility of interpreting and acting on a prophecy lies heavily on the seer and those who consult them.

Interpretation and Symbolism

The interpretation of visions and prophecies is a nuanced skill that takes years to master. Celtic seers often rely on a deep understanding of symbolism, mythology, and natural elements to decode the messages within their visions. For instance, seeing a crow might symbolize transformation, while a river might symbolize life's constant flux. It's a nuanced language, one deeply intertwined with the cultural and spiritual fabric of the Celtic tradition.

Additionally, interpretation often requires validation through other forms of divination, consultation with other seers, or through natural signs and synchronicities.

Ethical Considerations

The ethics surrounding visions and prophecies are complex. Since these visions can influence the choices of individuals and communities, the seer has a moral obligation to be as accurate and honest as possible. It's considered unethical to manipulate or exaggerate visions for personal gain or to intentionally sow discord. Also, confidentiality often plays a significant role, especially when the visions pertain to sensitive or personal information.

Balancing Skepticism and Openness

It's essential for both seers and those who consult them to maintain a balance between skepticism and openness. Not every vision is a profound revelation. Some might be influenced by the seer's subconscious thoughts or desires. Discernment, therefore, is key to distinguishing between authentic prophetic visions and those that might be less significant.

Being too skeptical could close one off to genuine guidance, while being overly credulous could lead to misguided actions. The goal is to approach visions and prophecies with an open heart but a discerning mind, allowing for the wisdom of the ages to illuminate the path forward without overshadowing personal agency and critical thinking.

In summary, visions and prophecies are a cornerstone in the practice of Celtic Seership. They serve as avenues for accessing deep wisdom, but come with their set of responsibilities and ethical considerations. Mastery in interpreting these visions is a lifelong journey, deeply rooted in the cultural, symbolic, and ethical fabric of the Celtic tradition. Whether you are a seasoned seer or a curious seeker, understanding the dynamics of visions and prophecies enriches the tapestry of experiences in the mystical realm of Celtic Seership.

CHAPTER 8: SACRED LANDSCAPES: STONE CIRCLES AND ANCIENT SITES

Seership doesn't exist in a vacuum; it's deeply intertwined with the land itself. In Celtic tradition, the Earth's features—mountains, rivers, forests—are not just passive settings but active participants in mystical experiences. Even more focused are the sacred landscapes: stone circles, ancient groves, and holy wells that dot the Celtic regions. These aren't merely historical landmarks; they serve as conduits for spiritual energy and act as meeting points between our world and the Otherworld.

The Resonance of Stone Circles

Stone circles like Stonehenge in England and the Ring of Brodgar in Scotland have captured human imagination for centuries. The precise arrangement of these large, often unwieldy stones suggests a deliberate effort to create a space for ritualistic or ceremonial purposes. Archaeological evidence suggests that these circles were constructed by Neolithic peoples, predating the Celts; however, they were appropriated and used by Celtic societies and their spiritual leaders, the Druids.

While the academic debate about their initial purpose is ongoing, what is widely accepted is that these circles resonate with Earth's natural energies. Seers and spiritual seekers often report heightened intuitive abilities when inside these stone rings. Some theories suggest that the placement of the stones aligns with astronomical phenomena, like the solstices or planetary movements, thereby harmonizing cosmic and terrestrial energies.

Holy Wells and Springs

Water is a universal symbol of life and purification in many cultures, and in Celtic traditions, it is no different. Holy wells and springs often become focal points for rituals that involve cleansing and healing. Many of these wells are believed to possess curative properties, validated through oral traditions and in some instances, historical documentation.

They also have a role in divination. For instance, it was a common practice for seers to gaze into the water to see visions or prophecies. A sense of reverence and awe usually surrounds these wells, often highlighted by the presence of votive offerings like coins, cloth strips, or small personal artifacts that are left by those seeking blessings or answers.

Forest Groves and Natural Sanctuaries

Forests and woodlands hold a particular fascination in Celtic myth and Seership. Trees like the oak, ash, and yew are revered not just for their material properties but for their spiritual significance. Forest groves often served as natural sanctuaries where Druids and seers conducted their rituals and meditations.

The seclusion offered by these groves provided a tranquil environment where spiritual energies could be more readily accessed.

Being in a forest grove, enveloped by the essence of the trees and the land, many seers feel a deeper connection to the Otherworld. Certain groves are even thought to be gateways to the Otherworld, making them powerful spots for rituals intended to bridge the two realms.

Human-Made Sacred Sites

Aside from natural landscapes, there are also man-made structures that are significant in the practice of Celtic Seership. These include ancient burial mounds, often referred to as "faery mounds," and standing stones or menhirs. These structures are believed to be charged with spiritual energy, either because of their age, their construction techniques, or the rituals performed there. Like stone circles, they serve as physical anchors for metaphysical activities, making them hotspots for visions and spiritual experiences.

Modern Reverence for Ancient Spaces

Today, many of these ancient landscapes are protected heritage sites, but their spiritual significance continues to be honored. Contemporary practitioners of Celtic Seership often make pilgrimages to these sites, seeking the wisdom and energies they are believed to hold. The surge in interest in Earth-based spirituality has led to a renewed appreciation for these sacred landscapes, not just as historical relics but as living entities that interact with those who approach them with respect and humility.

In summary, sacred landscapes form an integral part of Celtic Seership. They are more than just historical or natural sites; they are vibrant, energetic fields that facilitate mystical experiences. Whether you're standing amidst ancient stones or sitting quietly in a secluded grove, the land itself becomes a participant in your spiritual journey, offering its own form of wisdom and enlightenment.

CHAPTER 9: ELEMENTAL MAGIC AND SEERSHIP

Celtic Seership involves far more than visions and prophecies; it's a deeply holistic approach to the world that recognizes the interconnectedness of all things. Among these interconnections, the elements of Earth, Air, Fire, and Water hold particular significance. Seers have long utilized elemental energies to deepen their practices, cultivate wisdom, and achieve balance. This chapter delves into the rich relationship between elemental magic and the nuanced art of Celtic Seership.

Earth: The Foundation of All

In Celtic tradition, Earth is more than just the ground beneath our feet; it is the lifeblood of all creation, encompassing mountains, forests, and fertile fields. It is the element of stability, nurturing, and grounding. Seers often turn to the Earth element to establish a firm foundation for their practices, meditations, and visions. They may use earth-related objects like stones, bones, or roots in divination, grounding their insights in the tangible world.

Earth is also the realm of the ancestors, providing a conduit for wisdom and guidance. Ancestral spirits are believed to reside in barrows, stone circles, and other ancient sites tied to the land, allowing seers to form a deeper connection through Earth-based rituals.

Air: The Breath of Life

Air, the element of intellect and communication, plays a significant role in enhancing a seer's perception. It is considered the vehicle of thought and the medium through which messages from the Otherworld are conveyed. Breathwork, an important aspect of Seership, allows practitioners to enter altered states of consciousness, facilitating clearer visions and greater understanding.

In Celtic lore, birds are often seen as messengers between realms, embodying the qualities of the Air element. Seers pay close attention to bird omens, interpreting their flight patterns or calls as signs or messages. The whisper of the wind, too, can be a medium for divinatory insights, especially when the seer has attuned themselves to the subtle energies of the Air element.

Fire: The Catalyst for Transformation

Fire, associated with passion, will, and transformation, offers powerful tools for seers. Candles, lamps, and bonfires are common in seership rituals, serving both practical and symbolic purposes. Fire is seen as a purifier, cleansing spiritual and physical spaces of negative energy. Its transformative power is also harnessed for divination techniques such as scrying, where the seer gazes into a flame to attain visions or insights.

In folklore, Fire is also tied to the divine, often represented by gods and goddesses associated with the sun, hearth, and forge. By invoking these deities in fire-based rituals, seers aim to channel divine wisdom and inspiration into their practice.

Water: The Wellspring of Intuition

Water, with its flowing, adapting nature, is the element closely linked to emotion, intuition, and the unconscious. Springs, wells, and rivers hold particular significance in Celtic tradition, often seen as liminal spaces where the veil between worlds is thin. Seers frequently use water in their rituals, sometimes employing techniques like hydromancy, where they seek visions through gazing at the water's surface.

Water is also closely associated with healing, both physical and spiritual. Many ancient sites dedicated to healing are located near water sources, and seers often use water in rituals aimed at cleansing, healing, or renewal.

Balancing the Elements

A proficient seer recognizes the need to balance all four elements within their practice. This equilibrium aids in achieving a more comprehensive understanding of the self and the world, allowing for clearer visions and more effective interpretations. Some seers create elemental altars or use tools like elemental pentagrams to represent and honor each element.

Seers also understand that the elements are not isolated forces but interconnected aspects of the larger web of existence. By building a relationship with each element, they strengthen their connection to the natural world and, by extension, their ability to navigate the complexities of the Otherworld.

In summary, elemental magic is not just an optional facet of Celtic Seership but an integral aspect that enhances the seer's abilities and enriches their practice. By understanding and harnessing the unique attributes and energies of Earth, Air, Fire, and Water, the seer deepens their connection to the world around them, becoming a more attuned, balanced, and effective practitioner.

CHAPTER 10: FESTIVALS AND RITUALS: CELEBRATING THE CELTIC WHEEL OF THE YEAR

Celtic Seership is deeply intertwined with the Wheel of the Year, a cyclical calendar marking the natural ebb and flow of seasons. By engaging with these key festivals and rituals, one not only harmonizes with the natural world but also fosters a spiritual connection to the Otherworld. This chapter aims to guide you through the major celebrations, their historical origins, and how modern seers incorporate them into their practice.

The Eight Spokes of the Wheel

In traditional Celtic culture, the Wheel of the Year comprises eight key festivals, roughly evenly spaced. These include the solstices and equinoxes, known as the "quarter days," and the cross-quarter days, which are midpoints between the former.

Samhain (October 31st to November 1st): Samhain, which is also known as the beginning of the Celtic New Year, is the time of year when the veil that separates our world from the Otherworld is at its thinnest. This makes it simpler for seers to speak with spirits and get visions during this time.

Yule (December 20th to December 23rd): This winter solstice festival celebrates the return of the light, as the days start to grow longer again.

Imbolc (February 1st to February 2nd): At the midpoint between winter and spring, this festival venerates Brigid, the goddess of fire, poetry, and healing.

Ostara (March 20th to March 23rd): The spring equinox celebrates the renewal of life and is often symbolized by eggs and hares.

Beltane (May 1st): Focused on fertility and love, Beltane rituals often involve maypole dances and the lighting of bonfires.

Litha (June 20th to June 23rd): The summer solstice, the longest day of the year, is an occasion for joyous celebrations and connecting with the power of the Sun.

Lughnasadh (August 1st): Named after the god Lugh, this is a harvest festival where people offer the first fruits as thanks for the abundance of the season.

Mabon (September 20th to September 23rd): The autumn equinox serves as a time for reflection, gratitude, and balancing light and dark aspects within oneself.

Historical Origins

The origins of these festivals can be traced back to the practices of ancient Druids, Bards, and Seers. Often held in sacred landscapes like stone circles or groves, these festivals would involve rituals, feasting, storytelling, and divination. For seers in particular, these occasions were crucial for communing with the Otherworld and receiving visions or guidance.

Modern Celebrations and Seership

Today, while many people celebrate these festivals for their cultural and seasonal significance, those engaged in Celtic Seership find them as avenues for deepening their spiritual practices. For example, modern seers might use Samhain as a time for intense divination and ancestor worship, given the thin veil between worlds. During Ostara, seers may perform rituals to tap into the regenerative energies of the season, often incorporating tools like Ogham staves or runes for additional insight.

Personalizing Your Practice

While there are traditional ways to celebrate these festivals, it's also encouraged to adapt them to your individual seership practice. This might involve creating your own rituals that incorporate elements of divination, ancestor worship, or elemental magic. The aim is to find meaningful ways to engage with these key moments in the Wheel of the Year, thereby enriching your spiritual journey.

Ethical Considerations

When celebrating these festivals, especially if they are not part of your ancestral heritage, it's crucial to approach them with respect and a commitment to authenticity. Appropriating aspects of Celtic spirituality without understanding their cultural context is generally considered unethical. Therefore, educating oneself about the history and significance of these practices is essential.

In summary, the festivals in the Celtic Wheel of the Year offer powerful touchpoints for those engaged in Seership. By understanding their historical origins and engaging in modern-day rituals, you can deepen your connection to both the natural and the Otherworld. Whether you adhere strictly to tradition or personalize your approach, the key is to participate with intention and respect.

CHAPTER 11: CONNECTING WITH CELTIC DEITIES

Celtic Seership is a tapestry woven with threads of history, folklore, the natural world, and spiritual connection. Among these threads, perhaps one of the most colorful and impactful is the interaction with the pantheon of Celtic deities. These gods and goddesses are not just mythological figures; they are spiritual entities with whom seers have had profound interactions over millennia. Understanding these beings and learning how to connect with them could significantly deepen one's seership experience.

The Importance of Deities in Seership

In the Celtic tradition, gods and goddesses serve as archetypes and symbols, each carrying distinct attributes and qualities. Whether it's Cernunnos, the horned god of fertility, or Brigid, the goddess of hearth and home, each deity personifies a specific aspect of life or nature. These archetypes provide seers with a lens through which to interpret visions, offer guidance, and even gain specialized skills in divination or healing. Unlike in monotheistic traditions, Celtic gods and goddesses are not considered omnipotent. Instead, they offer a more localized or specialized influence, making them relatable and approachable for individual seers.

Types of Celtic Deities

The Celtic pantheon is rich and varied, emanating from different regions such as Ireland, Wales, and Scotland. Some of the prominent deities include:

Cernunnos: Known as the horned god, associated with animals, nature, and fertility.

Brigid: Goddess of fire, fertility, and poetry, often called upon for inspiration.

Morrigan: A war goddess known for her shape-shifting abilities, often appearing as a crow.

Lugh: Known for his skill in many arts, he's the god of light and illumination.

Danu: The mother goddess, often associated with rivers and water, she represents fertility and abundance.

Methods of Connection

One of the primary ways to connect with these deities is through ritual. Rituals could be as elaborate as group ceremonies performed at significant locations or as simple as individual prayers and offerings. Offerings might include food, herbs, or small tokens that have a connection to the particular deity. Some modern practitioners also use visualization meditations to seek communion with these beings, imagining vividly the settings in which these deities are usually encountered.

Another significant method of connection is through dreamwork, which has been explored in earlier chapters. Some seers believe that specific gods and goddesses can be accessed more readily in the dream state and offer guidance or insights pertinent to the seer's questions or life circumstances.

Ethical Considerations

When connecting with deities, it's essential to approach them with respect and integrity. It's generally not advisable to "command" a deity to do something for you; instead, think of it as forming a partnership. The relationship should be reciprocal. Just as you may ask for guidance or assistance, consider what you might offer in return, such as an act that honors that deity's specific domain.

Personalization and Modern Adaptations

While the ancient Celts had their methods and understandings of these deities, modern seers have adapted these connections to fit contemporary needs and worldviews. For example, some practitioners focus more on the archetypal qualities these gods and goddesses represent, instead of treating them as literal beings. Others integrate these deities into broader spiritual systems, including Wicca or general neo-paganism. The key is to find a personal connection that respects the tradition but also serves your spiritual and Seership needs effectively.

In summary, connecting with the Celtic deities adds another layer of richness and depth to the practice of Seership. Through understanding the attributes of these gods and goddesses, you can gain new perspectives and skills that can profoundly influence your abilities as a seer. Whether through rituals, offerings, or meditative practices, these connections offer a way to deepen your understanding of both the visible and the hidden worlds. So as you continue your journey in Celtic Seership, consider forging relationships with these ancient yet ever-relevant beings. Their wisdom and influence could be the guiding light you've been seeking.

CHAPTER 12: THE ROLE OF ANCESTOR WORSHIP

Ancestor worship and veneration play a unique and integral role in the fabric of Celtic Seership. This practice links the realms of the living and the departed, allowing a continuity of wisdom, guidance, and connection that transcends the barriers of time and space. In this chapter, we explore how the respect and worship of ancestors influence the practice of Celtic Seership, both as a source of wisdom and as a form of spiritual grounding.

The Concept of Ancestry in Celtic Traditions

In many ancient societies, including Celtic ones, the concept of ancestry goes beyond mere genealogy. Ancestors are seen not just as those who have passed on, but as eternal guides who maintain a symbiotic relationship with the living. In Celtic beliefs, the ancestors reside in the Otherworld, a realm that coexists with our own. This Otherworldly connection is considered vital to the well-being of individuals and communities.

Seers often act as intermediaries between the Otherworld and the realm of the living, making ancestor worship a natural extension of their role. Through various divinatory methods, seers can establish communication with ancestors to seek guidance, blessings, or even to intervene in earthly matters. Some seers claim to channel ancestors directly, while others interpret signs and omens as messages from these wise forebears.

Rituals and Practices

There are several ways that ancestor worship manifests in the practices of Celtic Seership. Altars may be erected to honor the ancestors, featuring offerings such as food, libations, and meaningful trinkets. Some practitioners use ancestral tokens, like family heirlooms or photographs, as conduits for communication during divination rituals.

Many seers include ancestral veneration as part of their yearly cycle, aligning it with Celtic festivals such as Samhain, where the veil between worlds is believed to be at its thinnest. Others maintain a regular practice, perhaps weekly or monthly, where they meditate on ancestral wisdom, offer gifts to the departed, or enact rituals to honor their memory and seek their counsel.

Ancestors as Spiritual Allies

Ancestors are often viewed as more than just deceased family members; they are spiritual allies who can provide a form of protective shield or guidance. According to the Celtic understanding, since ancestors have already passed through the cycle of life and death, they possess wisdom that is valuable for navigating earthly challenges.

However, the relationship isn't just one-sided. Ancestors are believed to benefit from the energy and offerings given by their living relatives. This creates a reciprocal relationship where the ancestors provide wisdom, protection, and blessings, while the living offer them energy, respect, and sustenance for their Otherworldly existence.

Ancestral Wisdom in Modern Seership

Modern practitioners of Celtic Seership have adapted the ancient practice of ancestor worship to fit contemporary spiritual landscapes. Many integrate family history research into their practice, attempting to know their ancestors better to establish a more concrete link during divinatory activities. Some even explore their ancestral lineage through DNA testing as a way to deepen their connection to those who have passed before them.

For those without a clear line to their own biological ancestry, or who are drawn to Celtic Seership without a Celtic lineage, the concept of "spiritual ancestry" often comes into play. Here, the practitioner may connect with historical figures, legendary heroes, or even archetypical ancestors who embody the wisdom and qualities they seek.

Ethical Considerations

While ancestor veneration is a highly revered practice, it's crucial to approach it with the utmost respect and sincerity. Exploitative or disrespectful practices can not only prove ineffective but can potentially harm the practitioner's spiritual well-being. Intentions must be clear, respectful, and aligned with the principles of honor and reverence that underscore the broader practices of Celtic Seership.

Summary

The practice of ancestor worship within the context of Celtic Seership provides a multi-dimensional spiritual experience that weaves the wisdom of the past into the fabric of the present. Through rituals, offerings, and divinatory practices, seers build a bridge between worlds, creating a channel for ancestral wisdom to flow. This serves not only as a source of guidance but also as a grounding practice that roots the seer in a lineage of wisdom that stretches beyond the confines of mortal existence. Thus, ancestor worship becomes a meaningful and integral part of the complex tapestry of Celtic Seership.

CHAPTER 13: MODERN SEERSHIP: BALANCING TRADITION AND INNOVATION

The journey through Celtic Seership is like traversing a spiral, where one revisits age-old traditions only to discover new layers of understanding. The modern seer finds themselves standing at the intersection of past and present, tradition and innovation. But how does one balance these seemingly conflicting elements? This chapter aims to offer insights into maintaining the integrity of ancient practices while adopting fresh perspectives that resonate with the times.

Revisiting Traditional Practices

Firstly, let's consider the importance of retaining traditional elements. Authenticity in Seership does not merely lie in keeping with the old ways but in understanding their essence and relevance. The rituals, divination tools, and invocations handed down through generations serve as the groundwork. They offer the time-tested wisdom that adds depth and dimension to one's practice. For example, the Ogham—an ancient system of writing and divination—remains a valuable tool for many modern seers.

Delving into ancient scripts and lores, participating in time-honored festivals, and connecting with sacred landscapes can all add layers of meaning to modern practice.

Adaptation and Personalization

Innovation in Seership is not about disregarding what has been established but about building upon it. Modern lifestyles, technological advancements, and evolving social perspectives can all contribute to how one approaches Seership today. For instance, many of today's seers find online communities a valuable resource for sharing insights and learning new techniques, which was unthinkable in earlier times. While tools like Ogham may remain constant, their interpretations can evolve. Moreover, the use of digital aids for divination or 'Digital Seership' has gained prominence, though it should be approached with the same reverence as traditional methods.

Ethical Considerations in the Modern Context

Ethics in Seership is another area that undergoes refinement as society evolves. For example, the increasing awareness of cultural appropriation has led modern seers to be more conscious of how they engage with practices from various traditions. The guiding principle remains respect—for the tradition, for the spirits and entities involved, and for the community of practitioners.

The Role of Technology

Many traditionalists may scoff at the idea of integrating technology into a practice as ancient as Celtic Seership. Yet, it's undeniable that technology has opened up new avenues for exploration and community-building. Virtual gatherings, online divination tools, and digital libraries of ancient texts offer accessibility that was previously unimaginable. While these can never replace the experience of physical rituals or the tactile sensation of divination tools, they offer alternatives that can be particularly beneficial in our fast-paced world.

Striking the Balance: Intuition and Mindfulness

The core of balancing tradition and innovation lies in developing a finely-tuned sense of intuition and mindfulness. These faculties guide one in discerning which elements to hold sacred and unchanging, and where there is room for adaptation. Intuition, cultivated through consistent practice and deep communion with the spiritual and natural world, serves as an internal compass. Mindfulness ensures that each decision is rooted in respect and understanding, rather than mere convenience or novelty.

Summary

Modern Seership stands at a fascinating crossroads where age-old wisdom can intermingle with the pulse of contemporary life. Far from being mutually exclusive, tradition and innovation can enrich each other in ways that make the practice of Seership more accessible and resonant. By holding the essence of ancient traditions dear, and thoughtfully incorporating modern understandings and tools, today's seer can have a rich, multi-dimensional practice that is both rooted and relevant.

Thus, the modern seer navigates through the ages, not by abandoning the old ways, but by letting each step on their path be informed by the wisdom of the past and the possibilities of the present. In this balance lies the continuity and vitality that keeps the tradition of Celtic Seership alive and ever-evolving.

CHAPTER 14: THE ROLE OF NATURE: TREES, ANIMALS, AND SPIRITS

Nature and the seer have an enduring, symbiotic relationship in Celtic tradition. This relationship extends not just to the majestic landscapes, but to individual elements within it—trees, animals, and spirits. Understanding the profound interconnectedness of all these elements can aid the modern seer in honing their skills and deepening their practice.

The Whispering Trees

In Celtic folklore, trees are not just passive elements in the landscape; they are sentient beings that possess wisdom and energy. The ancient Druids held groves sacred, often conducting ceremonies under the shadow of ancient oaks or yews. They believed that certain trees had particular attributes—oaks for strength, willows for emotional insight, and so forth. The Ogham alphabet, often used in divination, associates different trees with various letters, linking literacy with nature in an intricate dance.

For the modern seer, communing with trees can be an enriching experience. Practices include grounding techniques, where the individual imagines roots extending from their feet into the ground, connecting with the energy of the Earth through the tree. Others engage in tree whispering, a meditative practice where you attune yourself to the subtle energies and 'listen' to what the tree has to offer. Incorporating such practices can not only enhance your seership abilities but also foster a deeper bond with nature.

Animals as Spirit Guides

Animals have always had a special place in Celtic cosmology. They serve as messengers, guides, and protectors in both the mortal world and the Otherworld. The stag, for instance, is often seen as a guide to the Otherworld, while the raven is associated with prophecy and insight. Just as trees have their own characteristics, animals also embody specific qualities—courage, cunning, wisdom—that can guide a seer in interpreting visions or embarking on journeys to the Otherworld.

Modern practitioners may find that they have a particular affinity for a certain animal, often referred to as a spirit animal or totem. This animal serves as a lifelong guide, offering its particular form of wisdom and protection. It is not uncommon for seers to employ meditations, dream interpretations, or even shamanic journeys to discover and connect with their animal guides.

Spirits of Place: The Genius Loci

The concept of "Genius Loci" or the spirit of a place, is vital in understanding the Celtic connection between Seership and nature. Whether it's a tranquil grove, a rushing river, or a towering mountain, each has a unique energy—or spirit—imbued within it. By learning to tap into these energies, a seer can gain profound insights into the nature of reality and the interconnected web of life.

While some places may be naturally imbued with a strong spirit, others may require attunement through ritual or quiet meditation. The Celtic practice of creating a sacred space, often marked by a circle or other geometric forms, facilitates this interaction. This space serves as a meeting ground between the natural and supernatural, enabling a rich exchange of energies and wisdom.

Respecting Natural Boundaries

While the call to commune with nature might be strong, it's crucial to approach this relationship with respect and ethical considerations. Not every tree or animal wishes to be disturbed, and not every spirit is benign. Understanding the need for boundaries, both in terms of physical spaces and ethereal realms, is crucial. Just as you wouldn't enter someone's home uninvited, the same respect should be extended to natural entities. The practice of asking for permission, either explicitly or intuitively, before engaging in any interaction can go a long way in establishing a healthy relationship with the natural world.

Summary

The connection between nature and the seer is foundational in Celtic tradition, offering both a source of wisdom and a conduit for energies. By understanding the attributes of specific trees and animals, modern seers can gain a more profound understanding of their visions and experiences. Recognizing the spirit of a place can also offer valuable insights. As with any relationship, the interaction with nature should be based on mutual respect and an understanding of boundaries, ensuring a balanced and harmonious coexistence.

CHAPTER 15: ANIMAL TOTEMS AND FAMILIARS

Animal totems and familiars have played an integral role in the practice of Celtic Seership, serving as messengers, guides, and allies in both the corporeal and spiritual realms. Drawing upon ancient symbolism and primal energies, these animals enhance the seer's abilities to perceive and interact with the Otherworld.

The Symbolic Nature of Animals in Celtic Tradition

Animals in Celtic traditions are much more than simple creatures roaming the Earth; they carry deep symbolic meanings, each representing specific traits or attributes. For instance, the stag is often associated with grace and majesty, whereas the raven has long been connected with prophecy and wisdom. These symbolic meanings are deeply rooted in the oral traditions and sacred texts that have been passed down through generations.

Understanding these symbols can offer the seer a rich vocabulary for interpreting their visions and experiences. For example, if one encounters a serpent in their journey to the Otherworld, it could represent transformation or rebirth, depending on its context within the vision. The knowledge of these symbols is vital for a seer, acting as a lexicon for deciphering the messages that come from beyond the veil.

The Role of Animal Familiars

A step beyond symbolic representation, familiars are specific animals or animal spirits that forge a unique, personal bond with the seer. These are not mere pets but are considered spiritual companions, aiding in the seer's quests, both mundane and mystical. Some believe that the familiar chooses the seer, appearing in visions or dreams to signal their willingness to collaborate.

The presence of a familiar can serve multiple functions. Some enhance or amplify the seer's abilities, some act as protectors, while others might guide the seer through the intricacies of the Otherworld. The role of the familiar is often determined through ongoing interactions and rituals that solidify and honor the partnership between the animal and the seer.

Animal Totems: Community and Ancestral Connections

While familiars are generally personal, animal totems often serve a broader role, representing entire communities or ancestral lines. In some traditions, specific animal totems are revered by families or clans and are considered guardians or emblematic spirits that embody the collective wisdom and traits of that group. Rituals may be carried out to honor these totems, seeking their guidance or protection for the community at large.

These totems serve as a reminder that the seer is part of a larger web of connections, not only vertically across different realms but also horizontally, throughout their community and lineage. It reiterates the idea that while a seer may journey alone into the Otherworld, they are never truly isolated but are part of a greater, interwoven tapestry of existence.

Modern Interpretations and Ethical Considerations

In the modern age, the concept of animal totems and familiars has expanded to include a broader range of species, moving beyond those traditionally recognized in Celtic folklore. However, it's important to approach this expansion with sensitivity and respect for both the animals involved and the cultural contexts from which these practices originate.

Ethically, the relationship between a seer and their familiar or totem should be one of mutual respect and benefit. This is not a matter of 'using' an animal for personal gain, but rather engaging in a reciprocal relationship that honors the autonomy and sacredness of the animal spirit. Some modern practitioners extend this ethical concern to advocate for the protection and preservation of the species that serve as their totems, integrating environmental stewardship into their spiritual practice.

Summary

The presence of animal totems and familiars in the practice of Celtic Seership enriches the experience by adding layers of symbolism, personal connection, and community engagement. These animals serve not merely as symbols but as active participants in the seer's spiritual journey, offering guidance, protection, and insight. As we navigate the complexities of modern life, these ancient partnerships remind us of the interconnectedness of all beings and offer a profound avenue for engaging with the mysteries of existence.

CHAPTER 16: DREAMING THE CELTIC WAY: VISIONS AND INSIGHTS

Dreaming holds a pivotal place in the tapestry of human experiences. In the realm of Celtic Seership, the act of dreaming gains even deeper layers of significance. It transcends the boundary between the mundane world and the Otherworld, serving as a vital bridge between the seen and the unseen. In this chapter, we'll delve into the unique aspects of dreaming within the Celtic tradition, exploring how dreams act as a conduit for visions, messages, and insights from beyond the veil.

Dream States: The Gateway to the Otherworld

In many ancient cultures, including Celtic traditions, dreaming was considered a sacred practice that offered access to higher wisdom and spiritual insight. The Celts were particularly fascinated by the liminality of the dream state, a threshold experience between waking and sleeping where the veil between worlds grows thin. According to lore and texts like the Irish Imramma, which describe voyages to the Otherworld, dreams were a potent means of interacting with the supernatural.

Dream states have always been regarded as a form of "altered consciousness," allowing the seer to traverse different realms and dimensions. The Celtic notion of "An Saol Eile" (The Other Life) often includes dream encounters with gods, goddesses, and ancestral spirits. These experiences serve as conduits for guidance, inspiration, and sometimes, even prophecy.

Dream Symbols and Archetypes

In Celtic Seership, the imagery and motifs that appear in dreams are not random; they are fraught with symbolism. Animals such as the crow, the deer, or the salmon frequently show up in dreams as messengers or guides. Additionally, natural elements like rivers, trees, and stones also carry symbolic weight. The seer often looks to ancient texts and folklore to interpret these symbols, while also considering the individual's own life circumstances.

The use of archetypes, universal symbols recognized across various cultures, is also prevalent. For instance, the archetype of the "Wise Old Man" or "Divine Feminine" could manifest in dreams to offer counsel. Recognizing and understanding these archetypes within the Celtic context is vital for extracting the dream's wisdom.

Rituals to Enhance Dreamwork

Engaging in rituals before sleep can aid in gaining more lucid and meaningful dream experiences. Pre-sleep rituals might include drinking herbal teas known for dream enhancement, like mugwort or chamomile. Some seers also find it beneficial to meditate on an intention or question before drifting to sleep.

An essential ritual is the act of journaling upon waking. Documenting the dream immediately upon waking helps in capturing its nuances and subtleties, which may otherwise be forgotten. This "dream journal" can later be analyzed to find patterns, symbols, and messages that recur over time.

Prophetic Dreams and Divination

One of the most captivating aspects of Celtic dreamwork is the potential for prophetic or divinatory insights. Historical texts, like the Welsh "Mabinogion," are replete with examples of prophetic dreams affecting the course of events. In modern times, seers pay close attention to dreams that exhibit a particular intensity or clarity, treating these as potential glimpses into future possibilities.

Dream divination could also be a community affair. During certain festivals like Samhain, when the veil between worlds is considered to be at its thinnest, communities may share and interpret dreams as a collective form of divination.

The Ethical Responsibility of Dream Interpretation

As in all aspects of Seership, interpreting dreams carries an ethical responsibility. One must be cautious when interpreting dreams that involve other people or suggest future events. Sharing these interpretations must be done respectfully, only with the consent of those involved, and without causing unnecessary distress or alarm. The Celtic ethical framework, which emphasizes honor, integrity, and community responsibility, applies equally to the realm of dreams.

To conclude, dreams in the context of Celtic Seership are not merely passive nocturnal experiences but active spiritual practices that offer valuable lessons and insights. The dream state acts as a potent bridge between our world and the Otherworld, facilitated through symbolic archetypes, ritualistic preparations, and ethical responsibility. Like a loom of intersecting threads, dreaming weaves together the complexities of the human psyche, spiritual guidance, and prophetic wisdom, creating a vibrant tapestry that enriches the practice of Seership.

CHAPTER 17: ORACLES AND CHANNELING: MESSAGES FROM BEYOND

In the path of Celtic Seership, practitioners often take on roles that transcend time and space. They not only interact with the natural world, but they also serve as conduits for messages from beyond our earthly plane. This chapter explores the mysterious practices of oracles and channeling, ways in which seers receive and impart messages from other realms, including the Otherworld, ancestral spirits, and even Celtic gods and goddesses.

The Tradition of Oracles in Celtic Seership

In ancient times, oracles were considered individuals with a divine gift, capable of speaking prophecies or advice bestowed upon them by higher powers. These seers would often enter into trance-like states to communicate with other realms and return with valuable insights. In the Celtic tradition, the oracle often held a high social standing, much like the Druids and Bards. Oracles were consulted for important matters, such as warfare strategies, marriage alliances, and even agricultural timings. Although methods have modernized, the core essence of serving as an oracle remains ingrained in the practice of Celtic Seership.

Channeling: A Multi-faceted Process

Channeling, in a broader sense, is the practice of acting as a conduit for messages from entities in other realms. Unlike the concept of being an oracle, channeling is not solely predictive. It can involve imparting wisdom, healing energies, or simple messages of comfort and guidance. In Celtic Seership, channeling might involve connecting with nature spirits, fae, or deities of the Celtic pantheon to seek guidance or wisdom.

There are various forms of channeling practices. Some involve automatic writing, where the seer, in a meditative state, allows messages to be written through them. Others may use tools like crystals, pendulums, or runes to facilitate the channeling process. Regardless of the method, the key is to achieve a state of mind that allows a smooth flow of messages from another realm.

Preparing for Oracle and Channeling Work

Preparation for such deep spiritual work involves a set of ritualistic practices. Creating a sacred space is often the first step. In this sacred space, elements such as fire, water, air, and Earth could be represented to facilitate a stronger connection with the natural and supernatural realms. Offerings might be made to the entities the seer wishes to connect with, and incantations or chants could be employed to raise the vibrational energy of the space.

It is also crucial to establish spiritual safeguards. Ancient Celtic seers believed in the concept of 'geis,' a set of taboos or prohibitions that serve to protect one from harmful energies. Modern seers often use protective symbols, talismans, or prayers to achieve a similar effect.

Ethical Considerations

Being an oracle or a channel comes with a great responsibility. Ethical guidelines are essential in ensuring that the messages are received and conveyed with integrity. Most critically, consent should always be obtained when channeling messages that involve another person. Similarly, the seer should aim to remain unbiased, avoiding the temptation to interpret the messages according to their own beliefs or wishes.

Staying Grounded

Given the ethereal nature of channeling and oracle work, it's crucial to remain grounded. This can be achieved through regular practices like meditation, spending time in nature, or engaging in physical activities. The aim is to balance the otherworldly experiences with the mundane aspects of earthly existence.

It's worth noting that not every message from another realm will be clear-cut or easily interpreted. Therefore, it's advised to keep a journal to note down the experiences and messages received. Over time, patterns may emerge, and the meanings become more apparent.

Summary

Oracles and channeling are integral aspects of Celtic Seership that stretch the boundaries of our understanding of reality. They serve as a bridge between the tangible world and the mystical realms beyond, offering us glimpses of wisdom and knowledge otherwise inaccessible. By adhering to ethical considerations, preparing oneself thoroughly, and maintaining a balanced approach, seers can navigate this complex yet enriching domain with grace and integrity. Whether you're seeking to deepen your practice or are curious about the messages that lie beyond the veil, oracle and channeling work provide a profound avenue for exploration and insight.

CHAPTER 18: THE ROLE OF HERBS AND PLANTS

Celtic Seership has often been described as a practice intricately bound to the natural world. One of the less-discussed but vital aspects of this traditional path is the use of botanical elements, primarily herbs and plants, in the processes of divination, ritual, and connection to the Otherworld. This chapter aims to shed light on the historical and modern applications of herbs and plants in the realm of Celtic Seership.

Botanical Lore and Historical Usage

The knowledge and application of plants in Celtic tradition are not only confined to healing or culinary purposes; they hold a significant place in the realm of the mystical as well. Historical texts and oral traditions alike suggest that Druids, bards, and seers held a wealth of botanical knowledge. The Druids, particularly, were experts in the use of plants and herbs for various purposes, including religious ceremonies, divination, and even rites of passage. Mistletoe, oak bark, and yew were among the most revered plants, often associated with the divine and the liminal spaces between worlds.

Herbal Divination

In the practice of divination, herbs play an often understated role. Mugwort, for example, has long been used to aid in dream work and astral projection, a vital aspect of the seer's repertoire. Thyme is used to increase psychic awareness, and sage, perhaps the most commonly used herb in modern spiritual practices, has been employed to cleanse spaces and improve intuition. These plants are often used as incense, in sachets, or consumed as teas before a seer engages in divination processes. The aroma or essence of these plants helps to attune the seer's senses to the energies of the Otherworld, facilitating a clearer, more insightful divination experience.

Ritual Enhancements

Plants like elder, lavender, and rosemary are frequently used in rituals to promote different outcomes. Elder is said to ward off evil spirits, lavender is known for promoting peace and harmony, and rosemary is thought to offer protection and clarity. Incorporating these herbs into rituals, either as burning incense, anointing oils, or even as garlands and wreaths, adds an additional layer of symbolic meaning and energy to the proceedings. Many contemporary practitioners are rediscovering these uses and incorporating them into modern rituals, often through locally sourced or sustainably harvested materials.

Healing and the Otherworld

While not strictly related to divination or ritual, the healing properties of plants have a specific relevance in Seership. Plants like calendula, known for its healing attributes, or valerian, used for calming nerves, often make appearances in rituals designed to restore health or psychological balance. The belief is that these plants carry both earthly and otherworldly energies, and employing them in a focused manner aligns these energies for the person's benefit. This dual functionality further cements the role of plants and herbs in the broader practice of Celtic Seership.

Ethical and Sustainable Practices

In the contemporary practice of Seership, sustainability and ethical sourcing have become important considerations. Many traditional plants are now endangered due to overharvesting and habitat destruction. It is crucial for modern seers to either grow their own herbs in a responsible manner or source them from ethical suppliers. Given the interconnectedness of all life, a respectful approach to the Earth's resources aligns with the core principles of Celtic Seership, which values harmony and balance in all interactions.

In conclusion, herbs and plants offer a multitude of uses within the practice of Celtic Seership, serving as tools for divination, as enhancers in ritual work, and as connectors to both earthly and otherworldly realms. These botanical elements add depth and richness to the seer's toolkit, enhancing both the practice and the practitioner's connection to the natural world. From history to modern times, the role of botanicals remains consistent: a grounding, enriching force that helps navigate the intricate pathways of the Otherworld. As with all aspects of Seership, this knowledge comes with the responsibility to act ethically and sustainably, ensuring that future generations can also tap into this ancient wisdom.

CHAPTER 19: OVERCOMING CHALLENGES: ETHICAL CONSIDERATIONS IN SEERSHIP

The practice of Celtic Seership offers a rich tapestry of wisdom, visions, and connection to otherworldly realms. However, it is not without its ethical considerations and moral dilemmas. Just as any other endeavor that involves guidance and influence, the role of the seer demands a keen understanding of the responsibilities that come with the practice. This chapter delves into the ethical challenges and considerations that seers may encounter on their path.

The Responsibility of Interpretation

One of the first ethical considerations in Seership is the responsibility that comes with interpreting visions or messages from the Otherworld. When a seer receives an insight or premonition, it often arrives in symbolic or cryptic forms. The interpretation of these messages requires not only skill but also ethical discretion. Misinterpretation or miscommunication can have far-reaching impacts on people's lives, potentially causing distress or leading them astray. It is imperative for a seer to recognize the weight of their role and ensure they communicate their insights with care, clarity, and humility.

Confidentiality and Trust

The relationship between a seer and those seeking guidance is built on trust. This trust can be easily eroded if confidentiality is not maintained. As people often share personal, sensitive information in a divination session, seers must practice stringent confidentiality. Leaking or mishandling of such information is not just an ethical violation but also a betrayal of the sacred trust placed in the seer's hands.

Manipulation and Abuse of Power

The position of a seer can offer a significant influence over others. The potential for manipulation or abuse of power is a serious ethical concern. Whether consciously or unconsciously, a seer can impose their beliefs, desires, or fears onto others, leading them down potentially harmful paths. Being aware of this power dynamic and actively seeking to mitigate its risks is essential for maintaining ethical integrity in the practice.

Financial Ethics

Seership, particularly in modern contexts, often involves monetary transactions. This can be a sensitive area fraught with ethical pitfalls. Setting exorbitant prices, exploiting desperate or vulnerable people, and promising guaranteed outcomes are all ethically problematic behaviors. Seers must maintain transparency in their financial dealings and ensure that their fees are fair, equitable, and commensurate with their services.

The Dilemma of Harmful Visions

Occasionally, seers may receive visions that predict harm or adversity. Handling such sensitive information requires an exceptional level of ethical discernment. Should the seer share this information with the person involved, or would it cause unnecessary fear and stress? Is there a way to present the information that empowers the individual to make informed choices? These are challenging questions that don't have simple answers. A seer must weigh the potential consequences carefully and strive to act in the best interests of all involved.

Professionalism and Accountability

Ethical challenges can be mitigated through professional conduct and accountability. Abiding by a code of ethics, receiving peer reviews, and engaging in continuing education can provide seers with ethical guidelines and a support network for addressing complex dilemmas. Moreover, open dialogue about ethical considerations within the community can help evolve and refine the collective understanding of what ethical Seership entails.

In summary, the practice of Celtic Seership is a multifaceted discipline enriched by its historical depth and otherworldly connections. Yet, like any powerful practice, it comes with ethical challenges that must be conscientiously navigated. Understanding the gravity of one's role, maintaining confidentiality, avoiding manipulation, acting with financial integrity, and handling sensitive information are key ethical considerations that every seer should keep at the forefront of their practice. By doing so, they uphold the dignity and sacredness of this ancient tradition while ensuring it remains a force for good in the modern world.

CHAPTER 20: NAVIGATING TRANSITIONS: LIFE, DEATH, AND REBIRTH

The tapestry of life is woven with a multitude of threads: joyous beginnings, transformative milestones, and inevitable closures. In this chapter, we will delve into the intimate relationship between Celtic Seership and life's significant transitions, such as birth, marriage, and death. We'll explore how the wisdom and practice of Seership can guide us and others through these crucial phases, shedding light on the spiritual dynamics that operate behind the scenes.

The Rite of Birth: Welcoming a Soul

From the seers' perspective, birth is not just a biological event but a spiritual ceremony in which a soul chooses to incarnate into a specific life. The role of the seer in this sacred process is to sense the new life's unique energy pattern, which may offer clues about its destiny and purpose. Some practitioners even work alongside midwives to create a welcoming atmosphere for the new soul, using ritual, chanting, and sometimes specific symbols that relate to the child's anticipated life path. The birthing room becomes a sanctuary, a liminal space between the Otherworld and this one, where the seer assists in facilitating the smooth transition of the soul into its new earthly life.

Marriage: Union of Souls

In Celtic tradition, marriage is considered a profound spiritual union, not merely a social or legal arrangement. The well-known practice of "handfasting" exemplifies this, as couples' hands are tied together to symbolize their connection not only in this life but also across various cycles of existence. The seer often presides over these ceremonies, reading the energies and potentialities of the union. By tuning into the subtle forces at play, the seer can suggest the most auspicious times for the ceremony, identify potential challenges the couple may face, and offer wisdom on how to harmonize their spiritual and emotional bodies.

Transitions of Age: Coming of Age and Elderhood

Celtic seers also play a role in other significant life changes, like coming-of-age ceremonies and transitions into elderhood. The seer can offer rites that help adolescents understand their new roles and responsibilities and can guide elders into their new positions as wisdom keepers within their communities. Here, the seer acts as a mediator, helping individuals reconcile the changes in their earthly roles with their unchanging, eternal selves, offering rites, prophecies, or wisdom that can aid in this shift.

The End: Navigating Death and the Afterlife

Death is perhaps the most mysterious transition, a return to the Otherworld from which all souls originate. The seer's role here is both delicate and profound. In cases of impending death, a seer can assist in preparing the soul for its journey, offering comfort and spiritual insight to both the departing and their loved ones. After the passing, some seers engage in psychopomp work, guiding the deceased through the confusing terrain of the afterlife and ensuring their safe transition to the next realm.

It is crucial to note that in Celtic tradition, death is not the end but a new beginning. The concept of reincarnation is often featured, where the soul is believed to return in a new form to continue its evolutionary journey. The seer's insight into the cycles of death and rebirth can provide a comforting narrative for those grappling with the existential questions that death often raises.

A Harmonizing Force

The seer acts as a harmonizing force during these life transitions, mediating between the physical world and the deeper, spiritual dimensions of existence. They offer rituals, prophecies, and wisdom that align individuals with the natural and cosmic rhythms that govern these significant life events. Their work ensures that each transition is not just a physiological change but a soulful journey imbued with spiritual significance.

In summary, Celtic Seership provides a compassionate framework for navigating life's most significant transitions. From the joyous welcome of a new life to the solemn yet hopeful farewell of death, the seer brings a touch of the sacred to these pivotal moments. They guide us in honoring each transition not as an isolated event but as a part of an interconnected spiritual tapestry, reminding us that our lives are but single threads woven into the intricate design of the universe.

CHAPTER 21: THE PSYCHOLOGY OF SEERSHIP

The practice of Celtic Seership isn't merely rooted in mystical experiences or ethereal visions. It has a psychological component that intertwines with its spiritual aspects. Understanding this intersection between psychology and the ancient practice of Seership can help practitioners gain a more nuanced perspective on their experiences and abilities.

The Power of Archetypes

Carl Jung, a Swiss psychiatrist, introduced the concept of archetypes, which are universally understood symbols or themes that resonate deeply within the collective unconscious. These archetypes can often be found in the stories, myths, and practices of Celtic Seership. Jung also emphasized the importance of integrating these archetypal elements into one's consciousness for psychological balance. For a seer, understanding archetypes can be vital in interpreting visions, prophecies, or interactions with otherworldly entities in a way that has psychological depth and coherence. It makes the process not just a mystical experience but also a psychologically enriching journey.

The Role of Intuition

Psychological studies have shown that intuition, often described as "gut feeling," is a rapid, unconscious assimilation of information. Seership heavily relies on the cultivation and honing of intuitive skills. Intuition can be seen as a form of internal wisdom, a quick and ready insight that bypasses rational thought. The act of divining, reading runes, or deciphering the Ogham script, for instance, all require an intuitive understanding that extends beyond mere logic. Being attuned to one's intuition can enhance the practice of Seership by providing more accurate readings and deeper insights into the mysteries being explored.

Altered States of Consciousness

In psychological terms, an altered state of consciousness is any mental state / condition which is vastly changed from a normative waking beta wave state of consciousness. Seers often find themselves in such altered states during visions, dreamwork, or meditation. Techniques like rhythmic drumming, fasting, and even the use of sacred plants can facilitate these states, enabling the seer to journey into other realms or gain profound insights. These states are also subject to scientific investigation, particularly in how they may correlate with brain wave patterns, neurotransmitter levels, and other physiological markers.

Coping Mechanisms and Personal Growth

Many who practice Seership find that their visions and experiences lead them towards personal growth and better coping mechanisms. The act of Seership—whether it's interpreting visions, engaging in rituals, or connecting with other realms—requires a strong sense of self-awareness and emotional intelligence. Practitioners often report increased resilience, better stress management, and a deeper sense of peace, aspects supported by psychological research on mindfulness and self-awareness practices. This convergence of psychological well-being and spiritual practice can make Seership a holistic approach to life.

Ethical and Psychological Considerations

Finally, there is an ethical dimension to the psychology of Seership. The power to see beyond the veil comes with the responsibility to handle such knowledge wisely. The psychological impact of a prophecy, vision, or divined message on others should be considered with care. Unethical use can lead to manipulative behavior or exploitation, either consciously or subconsciously. Equally, practitioners should be aware of the potential for self-delusion or the projection of one's own psychological issues onto the reading or vision, aspects that are well-documented in the field of psychology.

In summary, understanding the psychological facets of Celtic Seership can provide deeper insights into the practice and its impact on the individual. From the role of archetypes to the importance of intuition, from the implications of altered states of consciousness to personal and ethical considerations, the psychology of Seership offers a complex and enriching layer to an already profound tradition.

CHAPTER 22: SACRED GEOMETRY AND SYMBOLS

Sacred geometry and symbols have long been instrumental in human understanding of the cosmos and the spiritual world. In Celtic Seership, these geometric forms and symbols serve as focal points for meditation, as visual representations of cosmic truths, and as tools for connecting with the Otherworld. Let's delve into how this venerable tradition incorporates these shapes and symbols to deepen understanding and broaden seership abilities.

The Spiral: An Eternal Path

The spiral is a common geometric shape found in nature, in galaxies, shells, and even the pattern of growth in plants. In Celtic symbolism, the spiral represents eternity, growth, and the cycles of life and seasons. It is also thought to signify spiritual journeys, the inward and outward paths of discovery and enlightenment. Seers often meditate on the spiral to attune themselves to the natural order of the universe or to gain deeper insights into their visions.

The Triquetra: The Power of Three

One of the most well-recognized symbols in Celtic art and spirituality is the triquetra, a three-cornered design that looks like three interlinked loops. This shape symbolizes the unity of three interconnected entities. For many Celtic seers, the triquetra represents the interconnectedness of Earth, Sea, and Sky, or the Triple Goddess as Maiden, Mother, and Crone. It can also signify the blending of past, present, and future. When used in meditations or rituals, the triquetra is believed to facilitate a balanced flow of energy.

Celtic Knots: Infinite Connections

Celtic knots are intricate, looped, and twisted designs with no clear start or end. These have various interpretations, but one common theme is the idea of interconnectedness and eternity. In Seership, Celtic knots often serve as symbols of the eternal loop of death and rebirth, the interconnectedness of all life, or even the labyrinthine pathways of the Otherworld. Seers may incorporate these designs into their tools, like staffs and talismans, or visualize them in meditations to focus their energy and intentions.

Ogham: An Alphabetic Oracle

While not a geometric shape, Ogham deserves mention here for its symbolic significance. It is an ancient alphabetic script, each letter of which is associated with a particular tree. In seership practices, Ogham staves—small sticks or pieces of wood inscribed with Ogham symbols—are commonly used for divination and to communicate with the Otherworld. The symbolic language of the trees, represented through Ogham, can offer nuanced insights into visions and queries presented by the seer.

Mandalas and the Circle of Wholeness

Though not exclusively Celtic, mandalas are often used in modern Celtic seership practices. A mandala is a geometric design that symbolically represents the universe. Often a circle enclosing a square with a deity on each side, mandalas can be an effective focus for meditation and are used to facilitate spiritual growth and healing. In Celtic Seership, the circle is especially relevant, symbolizing wholeness, unity, and the cyclical nature of life. When seers include mandalas in their practice, it's often with a Celtic twist, incorporating traditional symbols and shapes like the spiral or triquetra into the design.

In summary, sacred geometry and symbols serve as physical manifestations of complex spiritual and metaphysical concepts in the practice of Celtic Seership. Through meditation and ritual use, these shapes and symbols become gateways to deeper understanding, facilitating the seer's connection to the Otherworld and enabling richer, more nuanced visions. Whether it is the eternal loops of the Celtic knots, the unity of the triquetra, or the spirals that mimic the galaxies, these forms invite us to consider the intricate interconnectedness of all that exists. Their enduring power lies in their ability to encapsulate cosmic truths, giving us tangible means to access the intangible.

CHAPTER 23: THE IMPORTANCE OF MUSIC AND CHANTING

Sound has a long history as a conduit for spiritual experiences, and in the Celtic tradition, music and chanting hold a particular reverence. They serve as vital elements in rituals, meditations, and even divination, enhancing the seer's connection to the Otherworld and aiding in the manifestation of visions. In this chapter, we delve into the intricate relationship between sound, music, and the practice of Seership in the Celtic tradition.

A Historical Perspective

The Celts, known for their love of music and poetry, considered the harp an instrument of the gods. The bards, who were both musicians and poets, played an essential role in the social and spiritual fabric of Celtic societies. Their melodies and chants were believed to have magical qualities, capable of healing, inspiring, and even leading one to the Otherworld. In ancient texts like the Irish epic "Táin Bó Cúailnge," the music of the harp is described as having the power to heal wounds, induce sleep, and bring joy.

The Power of Vibrations

In both science and spirituality, sound is understood as a form of vibration. Every object, including the human body, has a natural frequency at which it vibrates. When a seer engages in chanting or listens to particular kinds of music, they are essentially fine-tuning their own vibrational frequency. This adjustment can enable a more harmonious interaction with the energies of the Otherworld, making it easier to receive visions, communicate with spirits, or practice divination.

Instruments in Rituals and Divination

Apart from the voice, various instruments have been traditionally used to aid in rituals and divination. The drum, flute, and, most notably, the Celtic harp are among these. Drums often accompany rituals aimed at journeying into the Otherworld, their rhythmic beating serving to induce altered states of consciousness. Flutes, usually made from wood, are played to invoke elemental spirits, particularly those associated with air and water. The Celtic harp, with its ethereal tones, is believed to open portals between worlds, serving as both a medium and a guide for the seer's quest into other realms.

Chanting and Mantras

Chanting, which is a common practice in many spiritual traditions around the world, has a special place in Celtic Seership. It often involves the repetitive utterance of words, phrases, or syllables considered to have magical or spiritual significance. Mantras might be invoked to call upon specific deities, elements, or ancestral spirits. In some practices, Ogham, the ancient alphabet of the Celts, is utilized in chanting to encode the vibrational essence of particular trees, stones, or natural elements into the ritual. The intonation of these ancient symbols serves to deepen the seer's connection with the natural world, drawing upon its energies for insight and wisdom.

Modern Adaptations

Today, with the advent of digital media, practitioners of Celtic Seership have adapted these ancient practices into new forms. Digital soundscapes that mimic the vibrations of traditional Celtic instruments, or even binaural beats designed to induce specific brainwave states, are increasingly popular. While these modern adaptations may lack the organic feel of traditional instruments, they offer a convenient and accessible way to integrate the power of sound into one's seership practice.

Incorporating Music and Chanting into Your Practice

If you're a novice or even a seasoned practitioner looking to enrich your seership practices, start by selecting music or chants that resonate with you personally. The key is to listen to your intuition; it will guide you toward the sounds that can help deepen your meditative or visionary states. Remember, there is no one-size-fits-all in Seership. What works for one person may not have the same effect on another, so take your time to explore different soundscapes.

In conclusion, music and chanting serve as more than just aesthetic or emotional elements in the context of Celtic Seership. They are powerful tools that can deepen your connection to the Otherworld, fine-tune your intuitive abilities, and enrich your overall spiritual experience. By understanding the historical importance and modern adaptations of these practices, you can incorporate the profound influence of sound into your own journey, enhancing both your perception and interaction with the mystical realms that lie beyond the veil.

CHAPTER 24: GENDER ROLES IN CELTIC SEERSHIP

Gender roles and their impact on spiritual and social practices have been subjects of discussion for centuries. In the realm of Celtic Seership, gender roles have been fluid, yet culturally influenced, through time. By taking a closer look at how gender has historically interacted with the role of the seer, we can gain insights into the evolving landscape of Celtic spiritual traditions.

Historical Perspectives on Gender and Seership

Celtic societies were often less rigid about gender roles than many other ancient cultures. Women could own property, lead tribes, and participate in battles. They were also involved in religious practices, and some served as Druids, Bards, and Seers. Early Irish literature and mythology offer instances of powerful female figures who had prophetic abilities, such as the Morrigan, a goddess of war and fate.

However, it is essential to note that while Celtic cultures did afford more opportunities and freedom to women, they were not entirely devoid of patriarchal influence. Male Druids were often more public figures, acting as advisors to kings and leaders, while female Druids or seeresses often worked in more localized settings, such as villages.

Modern Interpretations and Inclusivity

In contemporary practices, there has been a significant push toward inclusivity and a questioning of traditional gender roles. The revivalist movements of Celtic spirituality and Seership have often emphasized the equality of all practitioners, irrespective of their gender. Many modern Celtic seership practitioners identify with non-binary, gender-fluid, or other non-traditional gender roles, reflecting the evolving understanding of gender as a spectrum rather than a binary.

Feminine and Masculine Energies

While the terms "feminine" and "masculine" are traditionally tied to biological sex, in the spiritual context, they are often understood as types of energy or qualities that anyone can embody. For instance, feminine energy is frequently associated with intuition, receptivity, and nurturing, vital attributes for a seer. On the other hand, masculine energy is often linked to logic, action, and protection. A well-rounded seer would strive to balance these energies within themselves, irrespective of their gender.

Gender-Specific Rituals and Practices

Even as inclusivity grows, some rituals and practices are traditionally associated with one gender. For example, in ancient times, women often led rituals tied to fertility and the Earth, given their direct biological role in childbirth. Men, conversely, might have been more involved in rites of passage like hunting or warfare. However, modern practitioners commonly argue that these roles should not be restrictive and that everyone can learn from engaging in various forms of rituals and practices.

The Role of LGBTQ+ Community in Celtic Seership

It's important to acknowledge the role of LGBTQ+ individuals in the modern landscape of Celtic Seership. As society's understanding of gender and sexuality expands, so too does the inclusivity in spiritual practices. Many contemporary seership communities actively welcome LGBTQ+ members and offer space for exploration of spiritual roles beyond the traditionally gendered norms.

In summary, gender roles in the context of Celtic Seership have been both fluid and culturally influenced over the centuries. While there has been a level of flexibility in gender roles within Celtic spiritual traditions, patriarchal structures were not entirely absent. Modern interpretations lean more toward inclusivity, acknowledging the role of feminine and masculine energies within all individuals and breaking away from traditional gender-specific rituals. The ongoing dialogue about gender in Celtic Seership is a testament to the evolving, living nature of this spiritual practice.

CHAPTER 25: ASTRAL PROJECTION AND OUT-OF-BODY EXPERIENCES

As we delve into the more esoteric dimensions of Celtic Seership, it's hard to overlook the intriguing subjects of astral projection and out-of-body experiences. While these practices might seem to border on the mystical and ethereal, they have been an integral part of Seership since ancient times. Astral projection allows seers to navigate different realms, engage with otherworldly beings, and acquire wisdom that transcends the limitations of the physical body. Let's take a closer look at these captivating facets of the seer's repertoire.

The Astral Realm: A Parallel Universe

The astral realm is considered a parallel dimension where energy and thought forms exist independently of the physical world. It's a realm that is both inside and outside of our regular waking consciousness. In Celtic tradition, this might be seen as another layer of the Otherworld, where seers can gain profound insights and commune with spiritual beings. By projecting their "astral bodies" into this realm, seers access a different mode of perception, often bringing back vital information or spiritual enrichment.

Techniques for Astral Projection

There are numerous methods for inducing astral projection, and while modern practitioners might employ updated techniques, the core principles remain rooted in age-old wisdom. Relaxation and focused visualization are key components. The seer often begins by attaining a deeply relaxed state, sometimes facilitated by breathing exercises or meditative chants. Then, through focused intent and visualization, the astral body is released to travel freely.

Some traditional practices include lying down in a quiet space and visualizing oneself rising out of the physical body. This might be accompanied by the chanting of specific mantras or the use of ritualistic tools to guide the astral body's movement. Regardless of the method used, the emphasis is always on practicing safely and responsibly, ideally under the guidance of an experienced mentor.

Distinguishing Out-of-Body Experiences

Out-of-body experiences (OBEs) are closely related to astral projection but tend to occur spontaneously, often during moments of extreme stress, near-death experiences, or during meditative states. During an OBE, the individual feels as if they are observing the world from a vantage point outside of their physical body. Celtic seers value these experiences as they provide a unique perspective on reality, enabling the seer to view life events and spiritual matters with enhanced clarity.

Ethical Considerations and Precautions

The allure of astral travel can be tempting, but it's crucial to approach it with the same ethical considerations one would apply to other aspects of Seership. The astral realm is not a playground; it's a dimension rich with its own set of rules and entities. Respect for these entities and the realm itself is paramount. In addition, astral projection should not be used to invade someone's privacy or manipulate events in the physical world. Always remember, the ultimate goal is spiritual enlightenment and the betterment of oneself and the community.

Interweaving with Other Practices

Astral projection and out-of-body experiences can be integrated into other elements of Celtic Seership. For example, during astral travel, a seer might engage in divination, commune with the fae or other otherworldly beings, or even attend ancient rituals and festivals in the astral realm. Moreover, information or wisdom gleaned from these experiences can enrich the seer's abilities in elemental magic, visions, and prophecies.

Summary

Astral projection and out-of-body experiences extend the boundaries of what is possible within Celtic Seership, offering avenues for deeper understanding and spiritual enlightenment. These practices allow for a unique form of travel that bypasses physical limitations, enabling seers to explore other dimensions for wisdom, guidance, and personal growth. Whether you're a seasoned practitioner or a curious novice, these esoteric aspects offer enriching paths for those willing to explore beyond the veil of the material world. With responsible practice and respectful intent, the realms of astral travel can become an invaluable aspect of your journey as a Celtic seer.Chapter 26: The Future of Celtic Seership: Emerging Trends

In a practice as timeless as Celtic Seership, one may wonder what the future holds. Rooted in ancient traditions, yet continuously nourished by modern interpretations and applications, Seership is far from a static endeavor. This chapter dives into the emerging trends that are shaping the future of Celtic Seership, taking a close look at how the practice is adapting to the complexities and challenges of contemporary life.

New Media and Technological Integration

While tradition is a cornerstone of Celtic Seership, adaptation is equally important for its survival. The rise of new media platforms like podcasts, YouTube channels, and social media communities has drastically increased accessibility to seership knowledge. Digital spaces have created venues for the sharing of insights, experiences, and rituals that were once passed down in far more intimate settings. Moreover, technology like augmented reality could open new doors to interactive and immersive experiences of the Otherworld, albeit cautiously and respectfully.

Ethical Evolutions

As global consciousness evolves, so does the focus on ethical considerations within various spiritual and occult practices. Celtic Seership is no exception. There's an increasing emphasis on consent, mental health, and the responsible use of resources. The integration of ethical frameworks from both ancient wisdom and modern thought enriches the practice, ensuring it stays both relevant and respectful to all involved.

Urban Seership

The majority of people now live in cities, far from the isolated natural landscapes often associated with traditional Celtic Seership. This shift has prompted an evolution in the way Seership is practiced. Urban seers find innovative ways to connect with natural elements, whether it's practicing divination in an apartment garden or tuning into the rhythms of urban wildlife. The essence of Seership isn't tied to a particular geography but lies in the perceptual and spiritual relationship with the world around us.

Revival of Lost Practices

Academic research and archeological discoveries continue to unearth lost or forgotten aspects of Celtic culture and spirituality. As new information becomes available, practitioners of Seership often incorporate these rediscovered elements into their practices. This form of dynamic interaction between scholarship and practice enriches Seership, offering a more nuanced understanding of its historical complexities.

Increased Interfaith and Cross-Cultural Exchanges

Celtic Seership, like many spiritual traditions, doesn't exist in isolation. There's a growing trend of interfaith dialogues and cross-cultural exchanges, offering fresh perspectives and methods that can be integrated into the practice. Such interactions also provide opportunities for Celtic seers to offer their own wisdom to other spiritual communities, fostering a mutually enriching exchange of ideas and practices.

Eco-Conscious Seership

Lastly, in a world grappling with ecological crises, the deep reverence for nature that is inherent in Celtic Seership is becoming increasingly significant. Many modern seers are becoming involved in environmental activism, seeing it as a logical extension of their spiritual responsibilities. This trend aligns well with the ancient principles of stewardship and offers a potent blend of spirituality and practical action.

Summary

Celtic Seership is a living tradition that continues to evolve. From ethical considerations to technological advancements, from urban adaptations to the revival of lost practices, the future of Celtic Seership looks both challenging and promising. As practitioners navigate these emerging trends, the core essence of connecting to the natural and supernatural worlds remains constant. This ensures that the wisdom of the ancients continues to guide and illuminate, even as new paths unfold.

CHAPTER 26: THE FUTURE OF CELTIC SEERSHIP: EMERGING TRENDS

As we journey through the corridors of time, one constant that becomes clear is that nothing remains static; everything is in a state of flux. The same is true for Celtic Seership, which has weathered the winds of change while maintaining its essential nature. While the practice remains anchored in ancient wisdom, it also presents a remarkable ability to adapt to the sensibilities of each age. This chapter aims to explore the emerging trends in Celtic Seership, examining how modern advances and shifts in collective consciousness are shaping this venerable tradition.

The Role of Technology in Seership

In an age where smartphones and the internet have infiltrated almost every aspect of daily life, Celtic Seership is no exception. Online communities have sprung up as platforms for sharing insights, conducting virtual rituals, and even offering seership services. Although there's ongoing debate about the efficacy of digital tools for spiritual practices, technology provides a bridge that unites practitioners globally, thereby fostering a collective evolution of the practice.

The Intersection of Science and Spirituality

Recent years have seen a fascinating interplay between science and spirituality. Neuroscience is beginning to explore altered states of consciousness, indirectly shedding light on the experiences that seers describe. While science doesn't necessarily validate the metaphysical aspects of Seership, it offers intriguing parallels that enrich our understanding. These intersections create a more inclusive dialogue that appeals to a broader audience, merging the logical and the mystical in a harmonious way.

Eco-Spirituality and Seership

As environmental crises escalate, the role of the seer as an earth-centered spiritual guide is becoming increasingly relevant. There's a resurgence in understanding the importance of our connection to the land and the spiritual dimensions it holds. This ecologically-centered approach to Seership underlines the practice as a tool for stewardship, grounding it in ethical responsibilities towards the Earth and all its inhabitants.

Gender Fluidity and Inclusivity

The question of gender roles in Seership is undergoing a dramatic transformation. While the ancient Celts had complex views on gender and spiritual roles, modern interpretations are pushing the boundaries to be more inclusive. The tradition is opening up to individuals irrespective of their gender identity, allowing for a more nuanced understanding of the energies and archetypes involved. This trend respects individuality and embraces diversity, aligning with broader societal changes.

The Revival of Ancestral Practices

Modern seekers are turning back to their roots for wisdom, causing a resurgence in ancestral practices. While Celtic Seership is often individualistic, the growing emphasis on communal wisdom and the reverence of ancestral lines enriches the practice. This connects current generations to the wellspring of their heritage, imbuing their seership practices with a depth that spans across time.

In summary, Celtic Seership is not a relic of the past, frozen in antiquity, but a living, breathing tradition that continues to evolve. Technology, the merging of science and spirituality, eco-spirituality, gender inclusivity, and the revival of ancestral wisdom are shaping the landscape of modern Celtic Seership. These emerging trends serve to not only adapt the practice to the modern world but also to deepen and enrich it, ensuring that it continues to be a vital, relevant part of spiritual exploration for years to come.

CHAPTER 27: PERSONAL JOURNEYS: STORIES OF MODERN CELTIC SEERS

The tapestry of Celtic Seership is richly woven with both ancient wisdom and modern experiences. In this chapter, we take a step away from theory and delve into the heartfelt testimonies and personal journeys of contemporary practitioners. These stories serve as living proof that the art of Seership is not confined to dusty scrolls or bygone eras, but is alive and well in the modern age.

Stories of Connection and Discovery

Many modern Celtic seers describe their journey as one of profound connection to ancestral roots. For some, the discovery of Seership was like finding a missing piece of themselves, as if they had been walking around with an incomplete puzzle their entire lives. These individuals often recount how embracing the path of the seer allowed them to forge deeper relationships with the land, their ancestors, and even the Otherworld, adding layers of depth to their everyday existence.

Navigating the Contemporary Landscape

In contrast to the traditional pastoral settings often associated with Celtic Seership, a growing number of modern seers have emerged from bustling urban landscapes. Despite the concrete jungles that surround them, these individuals have discovered ways to practice Seership that are both relevant and effective. Virtual gatherings, online courses, and a plethora of digital resources have aided them in navigating their spiritual journey. For these modern seers, the essence of the practice remains the same; it's the tools and the mediums that have evolved.

Encounters with the Fae and Otherworldly Beings

No tale of Seership is complete without the often mesmerizing encounters with the Fae or other beings from the Otherworld. While the specifics may vary, a recurring theme in these modern stories is the profound respect and caution exercised during these interactions. Interestingly, many have noted how their experiences seemed to blur the lines between myth and reality, leaving them with more questions than answers, but also a renewed sense of awe and wonder.

Transformation Through Trials

Seership is not a path devoid of challenges; in fact, it is often fraught with them. Yet, it is through these trials that many modern seers find their greatest transformations. Whether it's the ethical complexities of revealing visions or the delicate balance of practicing in a world that may not fully understand or accept them, these challenges serve as rites of passage. They are the crucibles in which the seer's resolve is tested and their wisdom is forged. Many recount how they emerged from such difficulties with a clearer understanding of their role and responsibilities, both to themselves and to the world at large.

The Renewed Role of Mentorship

In a world saturated with information, finding credible and compassionate mentors has become both easier and more complex. A common thread among the stories of modern seers is the indispensable role played by mentors. Whether these mentors are met in person or virtually, the impact they have is often profound. They serve as guides who not only share invaluable insights but also provide emotional support and grounding, aspects often overlooked but essential in the practice of Seership.

In summary, the personal journeys of modern Celtic seers offer a kaleidoscope of experiences that echo the rich history and expand the future possibilities of this ancient practice. These stories inspire us to acknowledge the diverse paths that lead to Seership while respecting the common essence that binds all practitioners. They remind us that, in a rapidly evolving world, the wisdom and gifts of Seership are not only relevant but are vital threads in the fabric of human experience.

CHAPTER 28: ONLINE COMMUNITIES AND DIGITAL SEERSHIP

The digital age has fundamentally altered many facets of our lives, from how we communicate to how we engage with spiritual practices. Celtic Seership is no exception to this transformation. Today, online platforms offer novel opportunities for both fledgling and seasoned practitioners of Seership to connect, share knowledge, and deepen their understanding of this ancient tradition.

Virtual Circles: The Rise of Online Communities

Before the advent of the internet, knowledge about Seership was largely disseminated through face-to-face interactions, written texts, or closed communities. Now, the landscape has changed dramatically. Online forums, social media platforms, and specialized websites serve as meeting places where people from around the world can come together to discuss various aspects of Celtic Seership. These platforms have democratized access to knowledge, allowing people from diverse backgrounds and geographical locations to partake in discussions that were once limited to select circles.

Online communities offer a plethora of resources, such as how-to guides, video tutorials, and interactive webinars. They also allow for a more diversified range of opinions and interpretations, which can lead to a more nuanced understanding of Celtic traditions and practices.

Ethical Considerations in the Digital Sphere

While the internet offers a bounty of resources, it also presents its own set of challenges, particularly in the realm of ethics. Authenticity, the responsible sharing of sacred knowledge, and issues of privacy are concerns that every member of an online Celtic seership community should consider. As with any spiritual or occult community, there are gatekeepers who claim sole authority over the "right" way to practice. One must exercise discernment and critical thinking to navigate the complex web of information and opinions.

Digital Tools for Divination and Practice

The internet is not only a place for communication and knowledge sharing but also offers various tools that practitioners can use to enhance their seership activities. There are apps for Ogham and Rune divination, digital libraries of ancient texts, and even virtual sacred spaces where users can meditate and perform rituals. While these digital tools can't replace the tactile experience of traditional practices, they do provide a convenient and accessible way for people to engage in Seership.

Accessibility and Inclusion

One significant advantage of online platforms is the accessibility they offer to those who may have been marginalized or excluded from traditional seership communities. Individuals with mobility issues, those who live in remote areas without access to a community, or those who face societal prejudices can find a safe and welcoming space online. Internet communities have the potential to be more inclusive and can adapt more quickly to the evolving needs of their members.

Bridging the Gap: Combining Traditional and Digital Practices

As Celtic Seership continues to evolve, the key to a fulfilling practice may lie in balancing traditional and digital elements. Online communities should not replace physical communities, but rather complement them. They can serve as a springboard for real-world connections and a way to broaden one's understanding of this rich and diverse spiritual tradition. Hybrid practices that integrate both online and offline elements can enrich the practitioner's experience, offering the best of both worlds.

In summary, the internet has opened up new vistas for the practice and understanding of Celtic Seership. While it offers unprecedented access to knowledge, tools, and a global community, it also requires a mindful approach to navigate its complexities. By responsibly integrating digital resources into one's practice, practitioners can benefit from an enriched and diverse tapestry of Celtic wisdom. Online communities can be powerful allies in one's journey through Celtic Seership, serving as spaces of learning, support, and spiritual growth.

CHAPTER 29: ENVIRONMENTAL STEWARDSHIP AND SEERSHIP

The concept of stewardship—the responsible management and care of something, usually the environment or other resources—isn't new. However, it holds particular weight and importance in the practice of Celtic Seership. Given that Seership is deeply tied to nature and the land, understanding our responsibility toward the environment becomes more than just a modern ecological imperative; it becomes an integral aspect of the spiritual path of the seer.

The Reciprocal Relationship with Nature

Celtic Seership has always embraced the interconnectedness of all things, drawing wisdom from the patterns and rhythms of the natural world. Trees, stones, animals, and even the phases of the moon offer invaluable insights to the seer. This symbiotic relationship mandates a certain level of respect and responsibility towards these elements. In ancient times, it was common for seers and Druids to serve as advisors to kings and chiefs, often counseling them on the importance of harmony with the land.

It was understood that imbalances in nature could result in imbalances in the community, leading to famine, disease, or conflict.

Modern Ecological Concerns

Today, the urgency of environmental issues is more apparent than ever. Climate change, deforestation, and the loss of biodiversity are just some of the global challenges we face. While modern seers may not hold the same advisory roles to governments as their ancient counterparts did, their stewardship responsibilities are no less significant. Through intentional actions, advocacy, and education, modern seers are taking up the mantle of environmental protectors.

Sacred Spaces and Conservation

Many seers have a unique relationship with specific landscapes, often considered as sacred spaces like ancient groves or stone circles. These spaces are not just historical or archaeological sites but living landscapes imbued with spiritual energy. The practice of Seership often involves rituals and activities that honor these spaces, like the act of leaving biodegradable offerings or conducting clean-up activities. In this way, seers are aligned with broader conservation efforts, working to ensure the protection and survival of these sacred landscapes for future generations.

Sustainability in Practice

When discussing environmental stewardship in the context of Seership, sustainability is a keyword. Ritual tools, often sourced directly from nature, can be acquired and used in a manner that respects their origins. For instance, if a ritual requires the use of herbs, responsible gathering techniques that don't harm the parent plant or deplete local populations are employed. Animal parts used for totems or other practices are preferably sourced from naturally deceased specimens, or if that's not feasible, purchased from responsible and humane sources.

Spiritual Significance of Environmental Stewardship

For the seer, stewardship isn't just a physical act but also a spiritual practice. It's a way of giving back to the source of their wisdom and insights. Just as one might make offerings to the gods, ancestors, or spirit guides, making an "offering" to the Earth by way of conservation and sustainable practice is an expression of gratitude and reverence. This builds up a form of spiritual capital, deepening the seer's connection with nature and by extension, enriching their practice and visions.

In summary, environmental stewardship in the context of Celtic Seership is a multifaceted responsibility that marries ancient wisdom with modern ecological imperatives. It acknowledges the deep, spiritual relationship between the seer and the natural world, transforming what could be seen as mere resource management into a sacred duty. By taking an active role in environmental protection and sustainability, modern practitioners of Seership not only preserve the sacred landscapes and elements that enrich their practice but also contribute to a more balanced and harmonious world for all.

CHAPTER 30: CREATING YOUR OWN TOOLS AND RITUALS

The journey of Celtic Seership is deeply personal, enriched by both collective tradition and individual insight. While the lore and ancient texts provide a robust foundation, it is through your personal touch that practices truly come alive. In this chapter, we'll delve into how you can create your own tools and rituals, ensuring your path in Seership is genuinely reflective of your unique spiritual fingerprint.

Crafting Tools with Intention

Many traditional tools of the Celtic seer, such as ogham staves or rune sets, have been passed down through generations. However, there's a unique potency in crafting your own tools, as they become imbued with your specific energy and intentions.

Selection of Material: Whether you're crafting a wand, a set of ogham staves, or a divining pendulum, the material you select should resonate with you. Wood from trees like oak, yew, or hazel is historically significant in Celtic tradition. Make sure the material you use is sourced responsibly and respectfully.

Consecration: Once you have your raw material, the act of consecrating it sets it apart for sacred use. This can be done through various methods, including anointing with oils, charging under a full moon, or invoking elemental spirits.

Design and Symbols: As you work on your tool, you might choose to incorporate traditional symbols, glyphs, or sigils that resonate with your practice. For example, engraving the ogham symbols on your staves can connect them to ancient Celtic knowledge while personalizing the tool for your own journey.

Personalizing Rituals

Just as you craft your tools, you also have the freedom to design your own rituals. Rituals form the backbone of practice, creating the space in which the sacred and the mundane meet. Here are some key points to consider:

Framework and Structure: Though you're creating your own rituals, maintaining a general framework can help maintain continuity with tradition. A typical Celtic ritual might involve casting a circle, calling the quarters, and opening a portal to the Otherworld.

Innovation: While sticking to a framework, don't hesitate to insert your own experiences and wisdom. If a certain deity, ancestor, or animal totem has significance for you, weave that entity into your ritual narrative.

Sensory Elements: The use of sound, scent, and color can add layers of meaning to your rituals. Consider crafting your own incense blend or composing a chant that complements your intentions.

Recording Your Insights

Creating a personal Book of Shadows or a similar journal can serve as a repository for your evolving insights. Keeping a written record of your own rituals, divination readings, or spiritual musings helps in analyzing patterns and deepening your understanding over time.

Ethical Considerations

When crafting your own tools and rituals, always consider the ethical implications of your actions. Ensure that materials are sustainably sourced and that your practices respect the autonomy and dignity of other beings, seen and unseen.

The Essence of Authenticity

Your journey in Celtic Seership will be most enriching when it mirrors your unique vibrancy. Crafting your own tools and rituals doesn't negate the wisdom of the ages; rather, it enriches it, adding another layer of depth and nuance to an ancient, living tradition. Through personalization, you can carve out a space within the broader canvas of Celtic Seership that is distinctly yours. This authenticity not only benefits you but also contributes to the evolving tapestry of collective knowledge and practice. Therefore, don't hesitate to put your own stamp on the tools and rituals you employ in your practice, for in doing so, you honor both the tradition and your own individual path within it.

CHAPTER 31: SECRECY AND MYSTERY SCHOOLS

The lore and practices of Celtic Seership are deeply intertwined with traditions of secrecy and initiation. The role of secret societies and mystery schools in the preservation and dissemination of esoteric knowledge has been a cornerstone in the development of seership practices. In this chapter, we will delve into these veiled institutions and their roles in the history and modern manifestation of Celtic Seership.

The Veil of Secrecy

Historically, the teachings of Celtic seers were not openly discussed or made available to the general public. The reasons for such secrecy varied but commonly included the preservation of sacred knowledge, ensuring it was passed only to individuals who were deemed worthy and could handle the responsibilities that came with such wisdom. Ancient Druidic orders, the forebearers of later seer traditions, were known to be highly secretive, transmitting knowledge orally to safeguard it from being written down and potentially misused. This culture of secrecy also helped to maintain the power and status of the Druids within society, as their wisdom was considered a valuable asset.

The Role of Mystery Schools

Mystery schools served as the educational establishments where these secret teachings were imparted. The term "mystery" here refers not to something that is entirely unknowable but rather to truths that are hidden from ordinary perception and require initiation to comprehend. Such schools had a hierarchical structure with various levels of initiation, and as one progressed, they would gain access to increasingly complex and esoteric teachings. The initiation processes often involved rites of passage, tests of character, and the completion of certain tasks or challenges to prove one's worthiness.

The Importance of Initiation

Initiation served as a transformative process, aimed at readying the individual for the reception of sacred knowledge. It was not just an introduction to new information but an intense, often life-changing experience that included both spiritual and psychological aspects. By undergoing initiation, individuals were believed to become attuned to higher frequencies of spiritual energy and could more easily access the Otherworld, thereby enhancing their seership abilities.

Modern Manifestations

In today's context, while the need for secrecy has diminished, the concept of mystery schools and initiation has not entirely vanished. Modern Druidic orders, Wiccan covens, and various other neopagan groups often include elements of secrecy and initiation. Online platforms have made it easier to share information, but the importance of personal mentorship and experiential learning remains a key aspect of modern seership training. Some organizations even offer courses and initiations in a digital format, attempting to bridge the gap between ancient tradition and contemporary needs.

Ethical Considerations

With the ease of information dissemination in the digital age, it's essential to approach the tradition of secrecy with care. Respect for the sanctity and importance of secret teachings is crucial. One must also consider that what is shared publicly may be misinterpreted or misused. Ethical considerations include ensuring that teachings are not commodified in a way that devalues them, and that they are shared with individuals who approach them with the appropriate respect and intent.

In summary, secrecy and mystery schools have played a significant role in the history and development of Celtic Seership. The ancient traditions of safeguarding wisdom through secrecy and imparting it through initiation continue to influence modern practices. These age-old systems not only protect the sanctity of esoteric knowledge but also prepare the individual for the psychological and spiritual transformations required for advanced Seership. As the world continues to change, it's vital that these traditions adapt while maintaining the essence that has kept them alive for millennia.

CHAPTER 32: CHILDREN AND SEERSHIP

In many traditions, the early years are considered a time of innate spiritual sensitivity. Celtic Seership is no exception, where the inclusion of young individuals in the esoteric arts is viewed with a sense of reverence. This chapter will explore how children are introduced and integrated into the age-old traditions of Celtic Seership.

Early Sensitivity and Awareness

Children are often thought to have a natural openness to spiritual experiences, as they have not yet been fully enculturated into societal norms and expectations. The liminal spaces between sleep and wakefulness, childhood games mimicking the invisible, and even the innate understanding of animism (the belief that even inanimate objects have life or spirit) can be early indicators of a child's spiritual awareness. Some families who follow the Celtic path may notice these signs and choose to guide their young ones carefully, respecting both the child's innate understanding and the ethics of the practice.

Family and Community Influence

In traditional Celtic societies, children often grew up in communal settings, surrounded by elders, bards, druids, and other spiritual leaders. Storytelling, folklore, and interactive rituals provided a natural avenue for children to learn about their spiritual heritage. While modern settings may differ, the essence remains the same—community and family serve as the primary educators in the spiritual development of the child. Parents and guardians can introduce children to simple rituals, stories of the Otherworld, and the significance of natural elements, thereby planting the seeds of understanding and respect for the spiritual path they may choose to follow.

Ethical Considerations in Child Involvement

The inclusion of children in spiritual practices is a delicate matter and raises ethical questions. Consent, age-appropriateness, and individual readiness are factors that require careful consideration. It's crucial to adapt teachings and practices to be age-appropriate, ensuring they are neither overly complex nor potentially frightening. When introducing divination, for instance, guardians might prefer to use simple nature-based methods, such as reading clouds or interpreting the behavior of animals, rather than more complicated systems like Ogham or runes.

Structured Learning and Rites of Passage

As the child grows, structured learning and rites of passage often come into play. These rituals can range from the symbolic— such as a "first quest" involving a solitary journey into nature— to more formalized instruction under a seasoned seer or druid. These experiences serve not only to impart knowledge but also to instill a sense of responsibility and respect for the powers and entities with which they may interact. Such rites of passage often occur during key transitional phases such as puberty, providing an anchored spiritual context for the whirlwind of changes the young individual experiences.

Modern Adaptations and Accessibility

In our digital age, it's easier than ever for interested young people to stumble upon the world of Celtic Seership through online forums, books, or even social media. However, the virtual realm also poses challenges, such as the potential for misinformation or exposure to practices not suitable for their age. Here, the role of responsible adult guidance becomes even more critical, serving as a filter and a guide, helping the young navigate their spiritual curiosity in a balanced and ethical manner.

In summary, the introduction and integration of children into the traditions of Celtic Seership require a thoughtful, ethical approach that respects both the child's innate spiritual sensitivities and the depth of the practice itself. This involves a community-based learning environment, age-appropriate teachings, rites of passage, and vigilant guidance in the modern, digital world. Done well, this early exposure can lay a rich, respectful foundation for a lifelong spiritual journey in the realm of Celtic Seership.

CHAPTER 33: TEACHING AND MENTORING IN SEERSHIP

In the realm of Celtic Seership, the journey of a seer often follows a path from novice to master, illuminated by the guidance of mentors. While the solitary practitioner can, indeed, achieve a degree of proficiency, the advantages of a well-structured educational environment cannot be overstated. In this chapter, we'll delve into the importance of mentorship, the nuances of passing down wisdom, and how one can find suitable teachers or become one oneself.

The Role of Mentorship

The model of master-apprentice relationships isn't new and is prevalent in various fields, from craftsmanship to scientific research. In the sphere of Celtic Seership, this relationship gains added layers of sacredness. While academic and digital resources can offer a great deal of information, they cannot fully substitute for the wisdom gleaned from an experienced mentor. The mentor serves as a living bridge between tradition and modernity, often customizing the instruction to suit the specific needs, talents, and questions of the apprentice.

Apprenticeship Dynamics

Traditionally, apprenticeships in Celtic Seership were rigorous and intense experiences, full of rites of passage and milestone evaluations. In today's age, the duration and format of apprenticeships can vary, but the essence remains—the transfer of wisdom from an experienced seer to an eager learner. The curriculum often includes mastering divination tools, learning sacred texts, understanding the significance of natural elements, and much more. At times, mentors will challenge apprentices by pushing their limits, not just to test their skills but to catalyze breakthroughs in their spiritual growth.

Community Learning and Group Dynamics

It's important to note that learning is not always a one-on-one dynamic. Sometimes, it takes place in a community setting. Many modern-day Celtic seership practitioners form groups, guilds, or even online communities where shared learning occurs. These groups usually have senior members who guide discussions, answer queries, and sometimes organize workshops. The advantage of a group setting is the diversity of experiences and perspectives it offers, which enriches the collective wisdom. However, it's crucial to ensure that these settings maintain the dignity, integrity, and respect that the sacred art of seership demands.

Criteria for Choosing a Mentor

Choosing a mentor is a significant step that requires careful consideration. One must evaluate not just the mentor's expertise but also their ethical standing and compatibility with one's own learning style. Some mentors are quite formal and follow a structured curriculum, while others adopt a more relaxed, conversational style. Moreover, do make it a point to check if the mentor's teachings are aligned with the sacred texts and traditional wisdom that form the foundation of Celtic Seership. A responsible mentor will encourage questions, be open to scrutiny, and act with humility rather than authoritarianism.

Becoming a Mentor

As one advances in their practice, the idea of becoming a mentor might come to the forefront. This is a role of great responsibility, requiring not just a deep understanding of Celtic Seership but also a compassionate disposition to guide others effectively. Effective mentors are open-minded, patient, and keenly aware that each apprentice is a unique individual who may need tailored guidance. If you're considering becoming a mentor, ensure that you are willing to invest not just time but also emotional and spiritual resources to uplift your apprentices.

Pedagogy and Evolution

While it's essential to respect and maintain the traditional aspects of Seership, one must also be open to new methods of teaching and learning. Digital platforms are now enabling remote learning and mentorship. Moreover, modern pedagogical techniques, such as experiential learning, can be incorporated to enhance the educational process. Therefore, mentors and learners alike must be adaptive and willing to embrace changes that can enrich the field of Celtic Seership without diluting its essence.

In sum, mentorship is a cornerstone in the field of Celtic Seership that adds depth, nuance, and authenticity to the practice. Whether you're a budding seer in search of a mentor or an experienced practitioner contemplating mentorship, the relationship between teacher and apprentice holds invaluable potential for both. Through effective mentorship, the sacred art of Celtic Seership can continue to flourish, evolve, and enrich lives, ensuring that the wisdom of the ages is passed down in a manner that's both respectful of tradition and adaptive to modern needs.

CHAPTER 34: SEERSHIP AND THE WIDER OCCULT TRADITION

In the world of spirituality and mysticism, Celtic Seership holds its unique space, deeply anchored in ancient wisdom and cultural practices. Yet, it is essential to recognize that Celtic Seership is part of a broader spectrum of the esoteric and occult traditions that have existed throughout human history. This chapter delves into how Celtic Seership interacts with other mystical and occult practices, what they share in common, and how they differ, enabling practitioners to draw upon a rich tapestry of wisdom.

Common Ground: Shared Principles and Beliefs

A noticeable commonality among most mystical and occult traditions is the belief in an unseen, metaphysical reality. Whether it's the Qabalistic Tree of Life, the Eastern concept of Chakras, or the Otherworld in Celtic lore, there's a shared understanding that a realm exists beyond the physical. These systems also often employ symbology, whether it's runes, Tarot cards, or Ogham in Celtic Seership, to connect and interact with this unseen reality.

Another shared feature is the concept of personal transformation and enlightenment. Whether it's through Buddhist meditation, Hermetic alchemy, or the visions of a Celtic seer, the ultimate goal is often similar—to attain a higher state of consciousness and foster a deeper understanding of oneself and the universe.

Esoteric Practices and Their Tools

Each tradition offers its unique methods and tools for divination, foresight, and connecting with other realms. Where Celtic Seership may use Ogham staves and natural elements like water and fire for divination, Tarot cards and astrological charts play a similar role in Western occult traditions. Likewise, the use of mantras in Eastern practices can be compared to the chanting and vocalizations often employed in Celtic rituals.

Uniqueness in Community and Tradition

While commonalities exist, it's also important to honor the distinctiveness of each tradition. Celtic Seership is deeply rooted in the lore and landscapes of the Celtic regions, imbued with a profound connection to nature and the land. The rites and rituals are specific to this lineage and may not easily translate into other systems. For example, the veneration of Celtic gods and goddesses, the role of the Fae and Otherworld beings, and the importance of ancestral worship make Celtic Seership a distinct path within the wider context of occult practices.

Cross-Pollination: Learning and Integrating

For those interested in multiple paths, there is the potential for enriching one's practice through cross-pollination. For instance, someone rooted in Celtic Seership might find value in incorporating the meditative practices from Eastern spirituality to deepen their introspective abilities. However, it's crucial to approach this with respect and a deep understanding of each tradition to avoid superficial amalgamations or cultural appropriation.

Ethical Considerations

As with any spiritual practice, ethical considerations must not be overlooked. Integrity is a shared value across most spiritual traditions. However, the ethical guidelines may vary. While the Wiccan Rede's "An it harm none, do what ye will" provides broad ethical guidance in Wiccan practices, Celtic Seership places a significant emphasis on respecting nature and maintaining balance. Therefore, when venturing into different spiritual traditions, it's crucial to understand and respect the ethical framework inherent to each.

Boundaries and Limitations

Although enriching one's practice through learning from other traditions can be beneficial, it's also important to recognize the limitations. Each system of belief and practice has evolved in its own cultural and historical context. As such, not every element from one will fit seamlessly into another. Practitioners need to be mindful of these limitations to maintain the integrity of their primary practice.

In summary, while Celtic Seership is a unique and deeply rooted tradition, it exists within a broader milieu of mystical and occult practices that have both similarities and differences. For the practitioner open to learning, this presents an opportunity to enrich and deepen their understanding and abilities, provided it is done with respect, integrity, and a thorough understanding of each tradition's nuances. This broader perspective enables a richer, more informed practice that is both grounded in the roots of Celtic wisdom and open to the treasures found in the wider world of occult knowledge.

CHAPTER 35: CONCLUSION: NAVIGATING THE PATH AHEAD

As we draw this illuminating journey to a close, it's worth taking a moment to reflect on the rich tapestry of knowledge and experiences that make up the world of Celtic Seership. This timeless spiritual practice spans centuries, traverses realms, and connects us deeply to the world around us. It also continues to evolve, embracing the complexities and challenges of the modern age. If there's one takeaway, it is that the path of the Celtic seer is not static; it's a living tradition that grows and adapts, just as we do.

Cultivating Wisdom and Insight

One of the recurring themes throughout this book is the immense importance of wisdom and discernment. The ancient seers were held in high regard not just for their visionary abilities but for their deep understanding of the natural and supernatural world. Whether it is the significance of the Otherworld, the interaction with the fae, or the ethical considerations that come with the gift of foresight, the role of the seer is complex and multifaceted.

Traditional Roots and Modern Branches

The tension between tradition and innovation is another key aspect of the journey into Celtic Seership. While ancient texts and practices provide a sturdy foundation, the influence of modern psychology, online communities, and even new divination tools are reshaping the terrain. And yet, the core principles —connection to nature, honoring ancestors, ethical integrity— remain steadfast. Balancing the old with the new is a delicate act, but one that offers immense rewards.

Intersectionality in Celtic Seership

As we've seen, Celtic Seership doesn't exist in isolation; it interacts meaningfully with other spiritual and occult traditions. It also engages with societal issues like gender roles and environmental stewardship. This makes the practice not just a personal spiritual path, but a lens through which to engage with the broader world. Your journey in Seership can be enriched by studying these intersections and incorporating insights from other traditions and contemporary issues.

Ethical and Practical Challenges

Embarking on the path of Seership is not without its challenges. Ethical considerations can be complex, and the seer often walks a tightrope between different realms and responsibilities. Preparing for these challenges is crucial, as is ongoing learning and mentorship. This is a path that demands not just technical skill in divination or ritual, but also deep moral integrity and a sense of responsibility to both the seen and unseen worlds.

The Road Ahead

Looking forward, it's evident that the practice of Celtic Seership is entering an exciting phase. Advances in psychology are providing new frameworks for understanding visions and prophecies, while the digital realm offers new avenues for community and learning. But perhaps most promising of all is the resurgence of interest in ancient wisdom traditions as tools for personal and collective transformation. The future of Celtic Seership, like its past, is rich with potential.

In closing, your own journey into the world of Celtic Seership is a personal odyssey that can span lifetimes, realms, and even dimensions. Whether you are drawn to the wisdom of the ancient Druids, the allure of fae interactions, or the grounding force of sacred landscapes, the path you walk is uniquely yours. Yet, it is also part of a broader tapestry, one that connects all seers through time and space. By stepping into this fascinating tradition, you are both honoring a rich history and participating in the unfolding of a vibrant future. May your path be illuminated by the gifts of the sight, enriched by wisdom, and guided by the deep, abiding connection to the natural and supernatural worlds that is the hallmark of the Celtic seer.

THE END

Printed in Great Britain
by Amazon